Creative DISPLAY FOR YOUR HOME

Cover pictures: (left)Wood Brothers; (top right) IPC
Magazines/Robert Harding Syndication; (bottom right) Marie
Claire Idées/Schwartz/Thiebaut-Morelle.

Page 1 Elizabeth Whiting and Associates/Andreas von Einsiedel;
page 3 IPC Magazines/Robert Harding Syndication; page 4
Home Flair Magazine; page 5 (t,br) Eaglemoss/Graham Rae, (bl)
IPC Magazines/Robert Harding Syndication.

Based on *Creating Your Home*,
published in the UK by
© Eaglemoss Publications Ltd 1996
All rights reserved

First published in North America
in 1997 by Betterway Books,
an imprint of F&W Publications Inc.
1507 Dana Avenue
Cincinnati, Ohio 45207
1-800/289-0963

ISBN 1-55870-469-8

Manufactured in Hong Kong

10 9 8 7 6 5 4 3

CREATING YOUR HOME

Creative DISPLAY IDEAS FOR YOUR HOME

BETTERWAY BOOKS

Contents

USE YOUR CREATIVITY TO TURN
PLAIN WALLS AND CORNERS INTO
PRIME DISPLAY SPACE

SHELVING

The key to displaying your treasures is showing them to their best advantage, while keeping them out of harm's way. In addition to display, shelves serve a functional purpose.

D isplaying your treasured keepsakes and prized collections allows you to enjoy them on a daily basis and lends a personal, familiar character to your surroundings. Finding somewhere to keep all your possessions, and leave scope for your future belongings, is still an ongoing challenge in any home. To solve any shortfall of storage and space, a combination of functional and decorative shelving is an attractive solution.

There are basically two main types of shelving to choose from – fixed, wall-mounted systems, including self-assembly kits, all-in-one bracket-and-shelf units and built-in shelves, and freestanding, movable units. Shelving is made in a variety of materials to suit all tastes and budgets. The least expensive are the sturdy metal, wooden and plastic systems designed for offices and garages. Medium-price shelving is often made from chipboard or blockboard with a wipe-clean melamine coating or hardwood veneer. Solid timber and glass or clear acrylic shelving costs a little more.

Before deciding on the best type of shelving for your budget, you should assess what you want to store. Your choice of shelving needs to take into account practicalities such as load-bearing capacity as well as how well the shelves fit in with your decor. Most manufacturers provide guidelines on this, but always ask for information if you need it.

Take a look around your home for any underexploited spaces – alcoves, under the stairs or over doorways or windows, for instance – where you could fit a shelf or two. Accessibility is important too, both in terms of where the shelves are situated and how you arrange items on them. Frequently used items need to be within easy reach. Deep shelves are rarely an advantage, as the last thing you want is to be constantly moving one row of things so you can reach another.

The functional appearance of these shelves really suits the modern layout of the room. At the same time, the galvanized tracks and smart wooden boards provide useful storage and display surfaces.

WALL-MOUNTED SHELVES

There are three distinct types of wall-fixed shelving: self-assembly kits, lightweight all-in-one bracket-and-shelf units, and shelving built into alcoves. Most do-it-yourself stores stock a wide range of shelf boards, tracks and brackets. Useful accessories include clip-on book ends, grooved shelves for displaying plates, and corner shelves that enable you to run a continuous length of shelving around a room.

Wall-mounted shelving is either set or adjustable. If you are reasonably sure that the contents of your shelves won't change, there is little point in buying adjustable shelving. However, if you think you may want to extend the shelving or alter its function over time, an adjustable system is the most practical.

▶ Brackets as shelves
Corbel-style brackets make excellent mini-shelves for holding individual ornaments, pot plants or a vase of flowers. Several grouped in an arrangement on the wall can look extremely effective.

▶ Trim tracks
Adding an edge trim to the shelves and filling them with an assortment of objects turns an ordinary track system into a smart array of shelving over one wall.

▶ Upper glass
A single glass shelf, supported on two decorative brass brackets, provides a discreet surface for showing off anything from pictures and cards to flowers and ornaments.

SELF-ASSEMBLY KITS

Apart from being inexpensive, the great advantage of self-assembly shelving kits is that you can tailor them to any items you want to display or store, from cassettes to candlesticks, books to bottles, and arrange the shelves where and how you want them. Shelving and fittings are normally sold separately, allowing you to buy as much or as little as you like.

When you are planning to fit several shelves in a stack, always measure the height of the items you want to store, and space the gaps between the shelves accordingly. Whichever shelving material you use, your shelves must be well fixed and supported so that they do not come away from the wall or sag.

Brackets and boards Right-angle brackets screwed directly into the wall are commonly used to support shelves. A wide range of designs is available. With brackets and boards, you can devise all kinds of shelving arrangements – from covering a whole wall to simply putting up a single display shelf. The main disadvantage is that the shelving takes a long time to put up, as each board has to be individually levelled and each bracket screwed to the wall.

Track systems In this very functional form of shelving, tiers of adjustable, wall-mounted shelves are fixed to metal tracks with rows of slots punched along their length for fitting the clips or brackets that hold the shelves at any height. The major advantage is that once one shelf is level, all the others will also be automatically level. Unfortunately, the tracks tend to show up clearly against the wall.

◀ *Brackets and boards*
Regularly spaced L-shaped brackets and wooden boards form the basis of a strong, practical and attractive storage system in this kitchen.

◀ *The right track*
Adjustable track shelving is highly flexible. You can slot in shelves at any height with variable spacing between them. In this child's room the shelves are ranged round the head of the bed, providing ample storage for toys, games, teddies and books, and a place for the bedside lamp.

◀ *Invisible support*
These shelves are supported along their back edges by an ingenious wall-fixed strip. Note how a shelf across the corner becomes a useful desk.

9

◀ All-in-one
A simple bracket shelf unit with an integral towel rail fits neatly into a small bathroom. It's easily attached to the wall with only two screws.

▼ Floor to wall
These modern shelf units, that are fixed to the wall and floor, combine the stability of wall-mounted shelving with the mobility of freestanding shelves.

FIXED UNITS

With fixed, assembled units, you get the best of both worlds: you can fit the shelves to the wall in one go, and transport them as one if you move.

All-in-one brackets and shelves You can buy small, lightweight shelving units, combining brackets and a shelf or shelves, to screw to the wall. Such units are often designed to hold specific items such as jars of spices or videos. Some are decorative, others are more functional. Some designs incorporate other features underneath the shelf, such as a single drawer, a towel rail or curtain rail, and are excellent space-savers.

Stacked shelf units You can hang a set of shelves fitted into a frame on the wall. Modern versions involving lightweight frames supporting wooden shelves are floorstanding but need to be fixed to the wall at the top for stability.

POINTS TO REMEMBER

Check what the walls are made of before fixing up the shelves. On partition walls, screw the shelf supports into the timber uprights for weight-bearing strength, rather than use hollow-wall fixings.

❖

Use a wiring detector to check that there are no electric cables and gas or water pipes hidden in the plaster where you want to fix the shelves.

◣ Stacks of shelving
In its simplicity, a lightweight, wooden unit with three shelves is in keeping with an American country style of decorating.

▶ Alcove alternatives
A combination of wooden and glass shelving on either side of this fireplace illustrates the value of alcove space for storage and display.

10

◄ *Customized shelves*
A compact unit with
well-lit glass shelves is
tailor-made to fit into the
alcove above this worktop.
The individual shelves
are carefully spaced to
accommodate the specific
items on them.

▼ *Block shelving*
Dividing the shelves
built in along one wall
into cubicles like this
turns standard living
room storage into an
original design and
display feature in a
minimalist setting.

BUILT-IN SHELVING

Tailoring shelves to fill an architectural gap, such
as an alcove beside a chimney breast, an under-
stairs triangle or over a door, is an extremely
practical use of space. For the most exclusive
custom-built shelving that adds classical storage
facilities to a room, you should call in a joiner.
Then you can decorate the shelving with paint
finishes and shelf-edge trims, and add display
lighting to your own specifications.

As well as the track-and-bracket systems
already mentioned, the most common methods
of fixing alcove shelving yourself are listed below.
Wooden battening is the easiest type of shelf
support to fit along two or three sides of an
alcove. The batten is clearly visible, but you can
paint it the same colour as the wall so it merges
into the background. You have to measure up
and fit each shelf independently, because the
walls of the alcove are unlikely to be true.
Shelf-end supports, made from thin strips of
aluminium or steel fitted to the sides of a narrow
alcove, are an unobtrusive option for short
shelves that don't need to carry too much
weight. There are various types, ranging from
slotted metal strips with small studs which fit into
them to carry the shelves, to plastic or metal
studs that screw into timber lining the side walls.
Alternatively, you can fit a right-angled metal
strip on each side of the alcove – and along the
back for a heavy load – and either rest the ends of
the shelves on top, or buy a grooved shelf that
slides over the bracket and hides it completely.

FREESTANDING SHELVING

Freestanding shelving fits inside a wooden or metal frame, which you can either place against a wall or set up so that it projects into the room, forming a high or low-level room divider. You usually buy the shelves and supports together, either ready-assembled or as a do-it-yourself flat-pack, which is the less expensive option. In either case, they are highly transportable and can go with you whenever you move home.

Freestanding shelving takes up more space than wall-mounted kinds and is often more expensive because it needs a strong frame. But, it is flexible. You can easily add on extra sections when you run out of storage space and rearrange the units whenever you want.

Industrial shelving is perfect in a garage or a tool shed, but its uses don't end there. Robust and considerably less expensive than other types of shelving, you can install it in a kitchen, teenager's bedroom or even a living room. The frames are made from steel, thick battens of wood or brightly coloured plastic tubing, bolted together, and usually have adjustable shelving, available in a choice of several widths.

◗ *The dividing line between freestanding shelving and modular storage systems is often very fine. Integrating shelves with matching cabinets and drawers lets you hide some items and display others.*

POINTS TO REMEMBER

When you buy kit shelving, try to see a ready-assembled version beforehand to make sure it is well designed and sturdy – especially if you want to use it as a room divider.

❖

If you are buying more than one shelving unit, ask for the manufacturer's brochure to study the full range of accessories.

❖

To prevent too much dust collecting when you use shelving as a room divider, include some closed cupboard units at floor level.

❖

◢ *Four-tiered independence*

A freestanding stack of four sturdy wooden shelves on a strong metal frame makes a handsome and useful piece of modern furniture wherever it is sited.

◗ *A hint at tidiness*

For trendy shelving at a bargain price, a commercial shelving system fits perfectly into a teenager's room.

WAYS WITH SHELVES

A kit shelf is easy to assemble and put up – the fun part is dressing up the shelf so that as well as serving a useful purpose it adds designer style to a room.

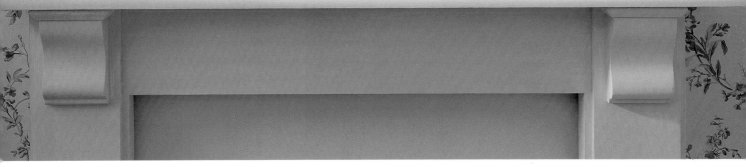

I n any house where space is tight, increasing the amount of storage will help to ease the squeeze. One of the best and least expensive solutions is to put up shelving, which makes good use of wall space as well as odd corners.

The easiest shelves to put up are those which come in kit form, ready supplied with bracket supports and all the necessary fixings. These basic shelves are available in different lengths, and you can also buy kits which include a peg rail to be fixed on the wall underneath the shelf itself.

Most kit shelving is made of unfinished pine which can be painted, colourwashed, stained or varnished before assembling to suit your room. Instructions for assembling and putting up a readily available kit shelf are given overleaf.

Once you have fixed up your shelf, you can go on to create original and eyecatching effects by dressing it up with wooden mouldings, dainty shells, paint effects or fabric. On the next few pages you'll find lots of inspiring ideas for decorating shelves which you can easily adapt for your home.

Three perfectly ordinary semi-circular shelves look remarkably stylish when painted a lively green to match the fireplace, and arranged in triangular formation like this.

PUTTING UP A KIT SHELF

These instructions are based on a readily available kit shelf, but you can easily adapt them for a different kit. If you are fixing the shelf on a solid wall, simply follow the instructions on this page. For a hollow wall, use special cavity fixings or screw the brackets directly into the wooden frame uprights that lie behind the wall. (Locate these by tapping the wall until you hear a dull sound.)

If you want to paint the shelf, do this before putting it up. Lightly sand down bare wood and paint on a coat of wood primer before painting.

1 Assembling the brackets Screw the two parts of each bracket together if necessary, using the screws provided.

2 Positioning the shelf Using a straight edge and spirit level, draw a horizontal guideline where you want the shelf to be positioned. Hold the shelf up to the pencil guideline, and mark the exact shelf length on the wall. To position the brackets, measure 6cm (2¼in) in from both shelf ends and mark these points with a pencil.

3 Putting up the brackets Hold one of the brackets up to the wall so the top and outer edge are aligned with the guidelines. Using a drill or bradawl, make a pilot mark through each screw hole. Hold the drill up to each pilot mark, and drill holes 2.5cm (1in) into the wall. Insert the wallplugs then screw the bracket into place. Repeat with the second bracket.

SHELF STYLE

Transform a plain kit shelf into a stylish and original piece of furniture by adding decorative wooden mouldings and a mottled paint effect. This is achieved by sponging a second, lighter colour over the first. Finally, give the finish depth and richness with gleaming gold wax, rubbed in to highlight the carved detail.

◀ *A pine kit shelf is sponged and gold waxed for an elegant antiqued effect which reinforces the blue and gold theme of the surroundings.*

▶ *Turn a shelf and peg rail kit into a focal point with a simple two-tone paint treatment. To ensure a neat finish, mask off the shelf edges, brackets and pegs when painting the main areas. When these have dried, mask them off to paint the rest.*

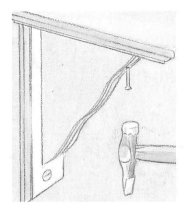

4 Fixing the shelf Rest the shelf on the brackets. Use the spirit level to check the shelf is horizontal, then nail it into place through the brackets.

1 Preparing the shelf Before assembly, sand down all the bare wood. Stick wooden motifs on to both sides of the two brackets with wood glue.

2 Painting the shelf Prime all the bare wood including the mouldings, and allow to dry. Lightly sand down all the surfaces.

▲ *Decorative wooden mouldings make a plain kit shelf look absolutely original. Do-it-yourself shops stock a range of designs in different shapes and sizes.*

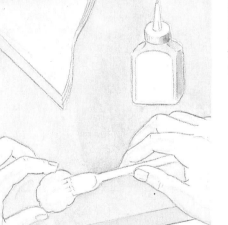

3 Adding colour Lightly sponge the dark blue paint over all the surfaces. Allow to dry. Repeat with pale blue paint, letting some dark colour show through. Leave to dry.

4 Antiquing the finish Using the tip of your finger, gently rub a little gold wax over the moulding and the bevelled edge of the shelf, to pick out the detail. Finally, assemble the painted shelf.

SHELF LIVES

Once you have painted and assembled your kit shelf, you can take your pick of decorative trims for the shelf edges. It's fun to experiment with different effects to suit a particular room or style of decoration.

The gingham frill illustrated on the right is ideal for finishing the edge of a small shelf in a country kitchen, while shells are especially appropriate stuck along the edge of a handy shelf in a bathroom. Depending on the decor, you could either leave the shells natural or make them shimmer with gold or silver paint.

To add a stylish individual touch to a new shelf in a bedroom, lightly glue a decorative braid or lace trim around the edges. A handmade lace or embroidery trim would suit the shelves in a romantic style bedroom. A length of brightly coloured ribbon or bobble fringing stuck round the shelf would liven up a child's room.

◄ *Ideal for a marine style bathroom, this kit shelf is simply decorated with glued on shells.*

▲ *A soft country style is achieved with a white colourwash over the shelves and a gingham frill attached with Velcro. Here, a lower shelf has matching curtains to conceal storage areas underneath. Terracotta pots and dried flowers complete the rustic look.*

◄ *You can buy ready-cut decorative shelf trims to jazz up a plain kit shelf. These are made of medium density fibreboard (MDF) and are simply held in place with glue or panel pins. Once the trims are fixed to the shelf edge, you can disguise the join by painting the whole assembly in a colour of your choice.*

Novelty Bathroom Shelves

Improving the look of your bathroom and increasing its storage capacity at the same time has to be a good idea. A few surprise tactics in your choice of shelving add a personal signature to a practical necessity.

An attractive shelving display helps to make a bathroom look less impersonal and starkly functional, and more in keeping with the rest of your home. Compact and largely private, a bathroom is also an ideal place to express the more flamboyant and adventurous side of your decorating talents – often the types of shelves you least expect to see in a bathroom have the greatest impact.

Open shelves are ideal for holding useful items that look good, such as colourful towels, prettily packaged toiletries or a flourishing house plant. If you keep items that you use everyday on the shelves, they need to be within easy access of the washbasin or bath, yet beyond the reach of curious young hands. On the other hand, when you just want extra surfaces for storing spare toilet rolls, soaps, powders or toothpaste, you can hang the shelves high up, making use of vacant wall space.

When your storage requirements are already well catered for by under or over the basin cupboards, you can concentrate on unusual shelving solely for display purposes. Book shelves or a plate shelf slot neatly into a bathroom for showing off china and glass ornaments or seaside memorabilia. If you fancy a very quirky type of shelving, have the courage of your convictions and follow your choice through by exhibiting an equally zany collection of curios on them.

A trio of leaping fish makes quite a catch as support for a small semicircular shelf in this aquatic theme bathroom. They look totally at home beside the cavorting mermaid and bathers, in the company of shoals of other fish, shells and starfish.

◢ A wall-hanging bookcase performs a novel role when put up in a bathroom to display a collection of seashells and pristine white china filled with flowers – plus a little light bathtime reading. A coat of sea-blue paint helps it to fit into its new watery surroundings.

◣ A pretty, old-fashioned shelf unit fits perfectly into a period-style bathroom, especially when it is flanked by a set of framed floral prints to match the flowery china, posies and pot pourri arrayed on the three tiers.

◣ An ingenious use of wicker panels as wide, open shelving hits just the right note in this modern bathroom. As long as they are kept neat and tidy, these honey-coloured shelves are the perfect place to stack clean towels.

◣ Miniature wooden shelves, with heart-shaped wire hangers, take up very little wall space and provide a quaint touch in a small, contemporary-style bathroom. Dividing the shelves into small compartments creates attractive niches for displaying tiny items in an orderly fashion.

ALCOVE SHELVING

Filled with books, ornaments, toys or whatever other items you need to house, alcove shelving makes a practical and colourful feature of a recessed space.

F itting shelves into an alcove is one of the best ways to use a valuable storage area that you might otherwise overlook. An alcove is usually too shallow to house a piece of freestanding furniture, but by building shelves into the space you can make use of the area without protruding into the room. Typically you would build alcove shelving on either side of the chimney breast in a living room, but you can fit it within any recessed space such as in an unused fireplace, where the chimney has been blocked off, or under the stairs.

With a supporting wall on either side and along the back, alcoves provide a perfect site for building shelves. The simplest and least expensive way of fixing them is to mount wooden battens around the three sides and secure the shelf on top. Otherwise you could fit another type of fixed or adjustable shelving support to the back or side walls. But be practical in your choice – some fixings may be inconvenient to fit, conspicuous or not strong enough.

You can position the shelves at whatever heights you need, depending on what you want to put on them. They can neatly accommodate a row of small paperback books and compact discs, taller illustrated books or display an attractive array of ornaments. If they are sturdy and deep enough you could even use them for heavy items such as a television or pieces of stereo equipment – in this case, keep them low for easy access.

Lining this alcove with a subtly printed wallpaper and fixing a decorative wooden trim to the front edge of each shelf creates an eyecatching display case for treasures.

FIXING ALCOVE SHELVING

These instructions show how to fix alcove shelving using batten supports. Before you start, measure the alcove and draw a sketch of its dimensions so you can position the shelves to fit your exact requirements. The sides of an alcove are not always parallel and the back wall may not be square, so it is wise to make separate templates and cut each shelf individually. Also, avoid fitting deep shelves in a shallow alcove, because the battens need to support the shelf for at least two thirds of its depth.

Ask your local lumberyard for help in choosing shelving materials strong enough to suit your purposes.

PREPARING THE PIECES

1 Marking the shelf positions Decide on the spacing of the shelves in the alcove and use a steel tape and pencil to mark the positions on one side wall. Using a spirit level and pencil, draw a horizontal line on the wall at each marked point.

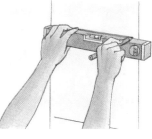

2 Marking the front edge Decide on the depth of the shelves. If they are all the same, use a plumb line to line up the front edge. Hang the plumb line against the side wall at the depth you want and mark off the front edge of each shelf.

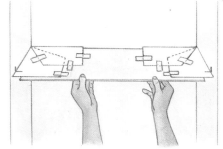

3 Making a shelf template As alcove walls are often not true, you may need to make a separate template for each shelf board. Use a piece of scrap board that fits inside the alcove. Working with a friend, hold the board at shelf level and tape pieces of card to the board so it fits the shelf space exactly, marking on the template each time where the front edge comes. For each shelf trace round its template on to a piece of shelf board and cut it out using a tenon saw.

4 Cutting the side battens For each shelf cut two side battens 5cm (2in) shorter than the depth of the shelf. If you want to bevel the front edge of the battens for a neat finish, hold each one firmly in a vice or clamp and saw off the front edge at an angle of 45°. Smooth the edge into a curve using a plane and sandpaper.

5 Making the drill holes Mark a screw hole 5cm (2in) in from both ends of each batten, and at 15cm (6in) intervals in-between if the batten is longer than 30cm (12in). Resting the batten on a piece of scrap wood, use the electric drill and a twist drill bit to make screw holes at the marks. Use a countersink bit to make a recess for the screw heads.

PUTTING UP SHELVES

1 **Fixing the first batten** Align the top edge of a batten against one of the lines marked on the alcove wall. Mark the position of one screw hole on the wall with a bradawl. Remove the batten and use a drill and masonry bit to make a hole in the wall at the mark. Insert a wallplug into the hole and screw the batten loosely in place. Lift the other end of the batten up until it is level, placing a spirit level on top to check. Mark through the other hole(s) and drill and plug as before, finally tightening all screws to secure the batten. Repeat, fixing a batten along each marked line.

2 **Lining up the second batten** Rest the appropriate shelf on its batten, place a spirit level on top and lift the other end until it is level. Hold a second batten under the shelf against the opposite side wall. Mark and fix the batten in the same way as in step 1.

3 **Adding a back batten (optional)** Add a back batten to shelves longer than 900mm (3ft) for added support. Measure the distance between the side battens along the back wall and cut a batten to this length. Drill holes in the batten as in *Preparing the Pieces*, step 5. With the shelf in place, hold the batten in position and mark the screw holes on the back wall. Remove shelf and secure batten as in step 1.

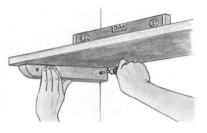

SECURING THE SHELVES

It is not essential to fix the shelf board to the battens but it does provide stability. Brass fittings known as mirror plates are best if the top of the shelf is visible; otherwise you can simply screw the shelves directly from above. To fit glass plates neatly, you need to make a recess in the battens using a chisel.

1 Fixing the mirror plates Use one mirror plate for each side batten and one or two for the back batten. Before fitting the side battens to the wall, chisel a shallow recess to take the mirror plate, midway along the top edge. Chisel recesses in the back batten. Screw the plates to the battens.

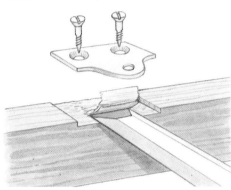

▲ *This series of slatted shelves, fitted into a former shower recess in a bathroom, is supported by battens on either side in the same way as shelving in a conventional alcove.*

2 Anchoring the shelf boards After the shelf board is in position on the battens, screw through the remaining hole in one of the mirror plates into the shelf board from underneath. Repeat on the other mirror plates. Secure the remaining shelves in the same way.

▲ *Painting this shelving to match its alcove surround disguises the batten supports and ensures it is perfectly in keeping with a formal drawing room.*

3 Finishing the shelves Cover the screwheads in the battens with wood filler. Prime the bare wood and then paint it, either matching the battens to the colour of the walls or to the shelves.

PLATE SHELVES

A plate shelf is the traditional means of displaying favourite plates and ornaments. Available in kit form, it is easy to put up and an instant way of providing more display space.

A plate shelf is basically an ordinary shelf with one or more grooves cut into it to hold the rims of plates, saucers and bowls securely in position to create an attractive display. For small collections, a single shelf is fine – fit it to the wall in a prominent position, above a table or similar focal point.

For larger collections, you can extend the shelf so that it runs all round the room. This looks dramatic, and provides plenty of extra storage space. Position the shelf at about picture rail height, so that you can reach the plates quite easily, without knocking them off accidentally. A good-looking alternative is to mount several shelves one above another.

In many ways, fitting a plate shelf is similar to fixing other mouldings – such as chair rails, picture rails and skirtings. The most important difference is the weight the shelf has to carry – china plates are not light. This makes it essential that you screw the shelf securely to the wall. The easiest shelves to put up are available as kits from do-it-yourself stores. You can also buy plate shelves as traditional mouldings from a timber merchant.

Once you have put up your plate shelf you can stain, varnish or paint the wood to suit the room. If you want to use varnishes and woodstains, it's a good idea to experiment on an offcut until you get the effect you want.

A plate shelf and a dresser provide complementary ways to display china. By painting the shelf the same colour as the wall, the objects on display become more eye-catching.

The kit usually has three main parts: an upright moulding that is screwed to the wall, a shelf secured horizontally to the top of the upright and a series of brackets that fit into the angle between the upright and shelf as support. Some kits also contain a packing piece, which is an extra strip of moulding that fits between the brackets for a decorative effect.

Consider the plate colours you want to display if you paint the shelf – here the blue of the shelf complements the plates.

YOU WILL NEED

- ❖ KIT PLATE SHELF
- ❖ TENON SAW
- ❖ ELECTRIC DRILL
- ❖ 2 and 4.5mm (¹/₁₂ and ³/₁₆ in) DRILL BITS
- ❖ COUNTERSINK BIT
- ❖ SPIRIT LEVEL
- ❖ 6mm (¼ in) MASONRY DRILL BIT
- ❖ WALLPLUGS
- ❖ SCREWS (with kit)
- ❖ SCREWDRIVER
- ❖ WOODWORKING ADHESIVE

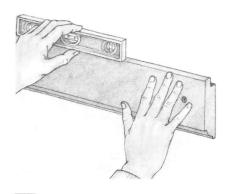

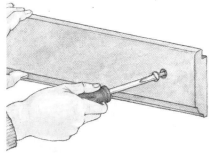

1 Sizing the shelf Cut the upright moulding to size. If you have to make a join, cut through two lengths of upright moulding squarely to make a neat butt join. Count the number of brackets supplied and drill a 4.5mm (³/₁₆in) hole for each one in the centre of the upright. Make sure the holes are spaced equally, at roughly 45cm (18in) intervals. Countersink the holes so that the screw heads sit below the surface.

TRADITIONAL WAY

Instead of a kit, you can use a length of upright moulding and a shelf with a groove running along its length into which the tongue of the upright moulding fits. Glue these two mouldings together using 25mm (1in) panel pins to secure the shelf to the upright. Glue brackets in place to support the shelf and cover up the screws that hold it to the wall. When continuing the shelving round a corner, scribe one length of moulding to fit over the other.

2 Positioning the shelf Hold the upright moulding up against the wall. Use a spirit level to check it is horizontal, and mark the position with a pencil. Now hold it up to the pencil line and transfer the position of the screw holes on to the wall by tapping a nail gently through each hole. Drill the holes in the wall and fit wallplugs.

4 Attaching the brackets Hook the brackets over the upright moulding, each bracket covering a screw. Cut the packing piece (if included in kit) into lengths to fit between the brackets. Glue brackets and packing pieces firmly in place and allow to dry.

3 Fixing to the wall Use 50mm (2in) No 8 screws to attach the upright moulding to the wall, tightening them fully and ensuring that all the screw heads are below the moulding surface. This allows the brackets to fit neatly on top.

5 Adding the top shelf Drill 4.5mm (³/₁₆in) holes every 60cm (2ft) along the top of the shelf, about 12mm (½in) from the back edge. Apply adhesive to the top of the packing piece and brackets, position the shelf on top of them and make 2mm (³/₃₂in) pilot holes. Screw down the shelf with 50mm (2in) No 8 screws and let adhesive dry.

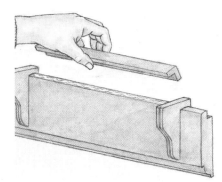

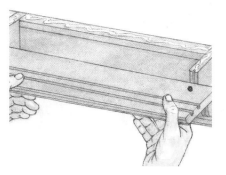

In a Supporting Role

By using your ingenuity, you can improvise some useful, inexpensive shelving from a few boards and a variety of everyday objects – and give your home a totally original look at the same time.

When you start looking around for objects to hold shelves, you find there are plenty of candidates. Stacked bricks, for example, make strong shelf supports, as do inexpensive, brightly coloured wastepaper bins. If you use sturdy pine packing cases as supports, you can turn the opening of the crate outwards and use the inside as bonus storage space.

It's fun to try and relate the shelf display to the improvised shelf supports in some way. For instance, you can use shelves held up by wine racks to display bottles and glasses in a dining room, or stacks of big books to carry book shelves in a child's room.

Even though these shelving ideas are quite impromptu, you still have to make the shelves as stable and level as possible. You also want to be confident that they are strong enough to carry the sort of load you expect them to. First and foremost, it's crucial to set up the stack of shelves on a firm base. For guaranteed stability, you should fill hollow items with stones or sand to make them heavier and less likely to fall over at the slightest knock. To ensure that the shelves are level as well as steady, you should always balance the shelf boards between identical items. Because these off-the-cuff shelving arrangements are freestanding, you're well advised to stand them against a wall, so that they can't get brushed against from all sides.

Richly coloured traditional wicker hampers or baskets adapt well to a new role, supporting a series of blond pine shelves. Such an arrangement looks absolutely at home in an apartment setting.

25

◀ *Large glass jars*, filled with pebbles or shells from a beach, become sturdy supports for a stack of bathroom shelves. By filling the jars with dried lentils, beans or rice instead, you can easily adapt the idea for shelves in the kitchen.

▶ *Terracotta flowerpots* make ideal spacers for a set of shelves in a conservatory or porch. It's a good idea to weight the pots with a few stones before erecting the shelves to give them greater stability. If you use planted strawberry pots to support the shelves, you can grow trailing plants in them to hang down on either side of your shelves.

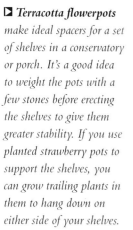

◀ *One good idea* leads to another when you use wine racks to carry shelves as well as to store bottles of wine. To steady the shelves, it's wise to keep a few full bottles in each rack at all times.

LEADING EDGES

*Polish up the look of plain shelves with a fabric disguise.
Shelf edgings, whether they are frilled, embroidered or shaped into pretty
scallops, add impact and instant charm to a shelf display.*

Soften the hard lines of a dresser, glazed cupboard or plain shelving with novelty shelf edgings made from fabric. The edgings, designed to drop down slightly in front of the shelf, are made in a vast number of ways using any material or trim that takes your fancy. If you like, you can extend the edging to cover the top of the shelf – a perfect solution if the surface needs protection or camouflaging

Ideally, for a cohesive look, the fabric used to make the shelf trim complements the items on display. For instance, dainty floral china may suggest a broderie anglaise or lacy trim, while bright pottery calls for a

bolder look of tartan ribbon. The shelving itself can dictate the edging you use – an antique dresser in dark timber benefits from a trim that is in period, such as lace, while brightly painted shelving suggests a more contemporary style of trim.

Once you have decided on the look you want, measure up the front edge of the shelves for the amount of trim you need. Ideally the edging should fold slightly on to the top of the shelf, so that it can be discreetly secured in place. You can use tacks, glue or touch fastenings to hold the edging firm, or you may find that double-sided tape is all you need to secure it.

Fresh yellow and white gingham, stitched into crisp, frilled edgings, suggests a contemporary country style. A second fabric in blue and white covering the shelves acts as a link to the blue wall behind.

■ *A deep zigzag* crocheted lace trim lightens up the sombre heaviness of this timber cupboard. The natural creaminess of the lace sets off the sparkling glasses and china beautifully.

▶ *A great deal of thought* has been given to these lively shelf edgings. Appliquéd motifs, in fabrics to echo the jazzy checked and plaid-patterned china, add a sense of exuberant clutter to the overall display. The edges of the trims are shaped into scallops and neatened with a self facing.

■ *Snappy stripes*, cut into a pronounced zigzag hem, bring a nautical feel to a carefully arranged display on open shelving. To copy this look, first back the fabric with iron-on interfacing, then cut it to shape and attach it to the shelves.

■ *Dainty embroidered linen* is an ideal trim for cupboard shelves displaying flower and fruit-patterned china. You can buy embroidered edgings that are deep enough to cover the whole shelf as well from fabric stores.

ON THE MANTELPIECE

Where better to keep a favourite clock or treasured ornaments, photographs and cards constantly to the forefront than prominently displayed on a mantelshelf?

L ocated on a projecting chimney breast, the mantelpiece over a fireplace is a natural focal feature of a living or dining room. Even in the absence of a fire, it is well worth retaining the mantelshelf as a conspicuous place on which to display a variety of cherished ornaments, mementoes and reminders.

Traditionally, symmetry is an important aspect of many mantelshelf displays. A pair of candlelamps or ceramic figures at either end of a mantelpiece, flanking a central vase of flowers or a handsome clock, forms a classically well-balanced arrangement for a formal living room.

Sometimes, an off-centred arrangement of objects is even more effective at catching the eye. A gradation from a tall black-iron candlestick at one end of the mantelshelf to a short one in the middle and a rounded vase or square picture at the other end makes a definite design statement in a modern apartment.

The mantelpiece is also the ideal location to set up a gallery of family photographs or an impromptu picture atlas of the postcards you receive from globe-trotting friends. By the same token, it's an unmissable place to stand invitations to weddings and parties as timely reminders of happy, forthcoming celebrations – these will heighten the anticipation every time you see them and guarantee that you don't miss any of the fun.

Treasured, fragile items, like a collection of precious, antique porcelain, are displayed well out of harm's way on a mantelshelf. Here the colouring of the china goes perfectly with the pattern on the tiles in the fire surround.

▶ A mantelshelf is the perfect place to show off a collection of novelties. In this case, a handsome clock sitting in stately splendour in the centre of a marble fireplace is joined by a cheerful tribe of gaily painted ceramic folk dolls.

◀ A well-balanced display of porcelain cats and trinket boxes in yellow echoes the predominant colour theme of the room. The best effects are always achieved when you relate the presentation on the mantelpiece to the style of the fireplace or the decor of the room.

▼ The choice of items in a mantelpiece display sets the mood. Here a quirky collection of unrelated objects and modern pictures helps a classically Victorian marble fireplace to blend in happily with the modern furnishings of the room.

▲ A decidedly white mantelpiece grouping grabs the attention. The informal arrangement of white china on a white mantelpiece against a white wall is brightened up by sunny splashes of yellow in the flowers and candles.

GLASS DISPLAY CASES

*Glass display cases are an elegant platform on which
to show off favourite ornaments and cherished collections,
free from curious hands, dirt and dust.*

D isplay cases fitted with glass panels all round allow your treasures to be viewed from all angles, as well as keeping them dust-free and out of harm's way. They also take up far less visual space than a display cabinet with solid sides and back, making them an excellent choice for small rooms. Light passes right through the case, adding extra sparkle to displays of glass and silverware and silhouetting each ornament. Choose a display case with glass shelves and your treasures will seem to float in mid-air.

Most glass display cases have an elegant frame, usually in wood or sometimes metal, which you can paint to match the surrounding decor or to tone with a colour-themed display. You might opt for a

stripped pine, limed wood or pastel-painted frame to complement a display of fine porcelain or glassware in an airy, soft modern scheme; or go for a bright gloss-painted metal frame to set off a collection of contemporary ornaments in a high-tech decor.

Glass cases needn't be reserved for display purposes – you can use them for storage too, provided you keep the contents tidy. Their transparency is an asset if you want to find what you're looking for quickly, whether it's crockery in the kitchen or towels and soap in the bathroom. In small rooms, consider using several cases placed side by side as an alternative to standard fitted storage cupboards – they give a much lighter, airier impression.

Three pastel-hued glass display cases stand tall and elegant between the windows of this informal living room, where rays of sunlight can work their magic on the treasures contained within – clear and frosted glassware, curvaceous pottery and gleaming silverware.

◀ *An ideal kitchen companion,* this blue lacquered display case slots in neatly to provide smart storage for everyday kitchenware.

▲ *Handsome and imposing,* a large rust-painted glass case echoes the rich tones of its magnificent display of glassware.

▲ *For storage purposes* in a small bathroom, a glass display case is hard to beat. It suits the streamlined decor, takes up little visual space and lets you see at a glance what you're looking for.

▶ *The warm tones* of a stripped pine display case are a perfect foil for the pink-tinged glassware and tablelinen it contains, as well as complementing the surrounding decor. Fresh flowers placed inside are a charming finishing touch.

LADDER DISPLAYS

As well as being essential items for household maintenance, ladders can also be used as handsome storage and display structures.

L adders, like many household items, have a striking form which is often overlooked because of their ordinary functions and cheap cost. While it's sensible to keep a ladder tucked away and instantly available for domestic use, a second and even third ladder can act as an eminently visible display and/or storage structure. Their geometric silhouettes and parallel horizontal steps form a lively rhythm, ideal for displaying a range of items.

Ladders can be made from wood or metal in styles ranging from elegant, Shaker-like simplicity to nostalgic rustic-work or streamlined high-tech, so keep the decor in mind when choosing one. Stepladders are usually free standing and can have as few as three steps, while extendible ladders need to be supported and can be several metres high.

For a contemporary look, colourwash a wooden ladder to tone with a room, perhaps stencilling the sides. Position it in a prominent place and display favourite ornaments, a vase of fresh cut flowers or a collection of pottery on the steps. If the ladder needs wall support, make sure it is firmly secured and won't slip.

Alternatively, for a country-style effect, suspend a rustic wooden ladder horizontally from the kitchen ceiling and hang bunches of dried flowers, strings of garlic, tea towels, utensils and even saucepans from the rungs.

An old ladder of turned, varnished wood is excellent for storing and displaying household linen. For a permanent display, you can screw ladders needing wall support securely to the wall.

33

◀ *Dizzy heights* are seemingly reached by this pale blue-stained, tapered ladder. These ladders were traditionally used by window cleaners and fruit pickers.

▼ *Making a perfect pair,* this quilt and hand-crafted, stripped wood ladder are Pennsylvania Dutch in spirit but equally suited to an English country cottage look.

▼ *Try a pair of stepladders* for tiered plant stands with an unpretentious appeal. Place an arching or trailing plant such as asparagus fern, spider plant or ivy on the top step.

CONSOLE TABLES

A console table is an elegant piece of furniture which fits perfectly into the living room or a hallway. Use it for displaying your treasured ornaments or as an original telephone table.

The graceful console table was a fashionable piece of furniture in the eighteenth century. It was originally a shelf-like structure fixed to a wall and supported by brackets or one or two legs. Today this style has been adapted for modern living, and while authentic styles which still need fixing to the wall exist, the more readily available versions are likely to be freestanding. They are still, however, ideal for positioning against the wall.

There is a place for console tables in any setting, whether in a country house or a modern apartment. They are perfect in hallways as elegant tele-phone tables. Alternatively, they are just as useful and stylish in a living room as an attractive display surface for a collection of ornaments, a china bowl filled with flowering bulbs or a vase of freshly cut flowers flanked with fine candle lamps.

Tables are either traditionally styled in dark, polished wood with a rectangular shape, or with a more modern look in unbleached or colourwashed wood and a softer, rounded outline. They may or may not have drawers. Table tops are generally covered with a fitted sheet of toughened glass to protect the surface.

An Art Deco-style console table, with its gracefully tapering legs, makes a fine focal point in a hallway. It is the perfect place to sit an old-fashioned telephone and urn-shaped lamp.

▶ *A sleekly modern interpretation* of a console table in pale wood works well in this contemporary apartment.

◀ *Colourwashed for a rustic look,* this old table provides the perfect setting for a vase of vibrant red amaryllis and cheery knick-knacks.

▼ *A variation on a theme,* a pale table with attractive bowed legs and slim drawers is perfect placed against a window. The pottery is shown off to full advantage in this brightly lit position.

▼ *Elegant and classic*, a reproduction hall table echoes the fine lines and perennial charms of the earlier console tables. Further the look by hanging a matching wooden-framed mirror above it and placing candle lamps on either side.

FOLDING TABLES

Portable, practical and easy to put up, small folding tables are perfect for display and for meals in front of the television, in the garden or in bed.

F olding wooden tables are modest but useful accessories, providing portable, stable, level surfaces for meals, card or board games and handicrafts or pastimes such as jigsaw puzzles. Folding tables can also be given permanent status as occasional tables, for displaying flower arrangements, lamps, magazines and ornaments.

Small, wooden folding tables are available as flat-packs from chain furniture stores and mail-order catalogues; look in secondhand shops for older styles such as traditional butler's-tray tables. If you're keen on antiques, there are examples of folding tables going back to the late 17th century; folding card, work and tea tables, mostly half-moon or rectangular in shape and opening out to reveal a baize or polished wood surface, featured in most Georgian and Victorian living rooms.

Whatever the age and style, test for stability before buying. You can personalize a plain wooden table by staining, stencilling or hand painting it to match the decor, or gluing on decoupage, then varnishing. Alternatively, choose a tablecloth that complements your room scheme.

Consider storing folding tables that are not in use Shaker-style, hung from wall hooks. Bear in mind, however, that wherever they are stored, folding tables should be quickly and easily accessible, otherwise they will remain unused.

This Victorian-style butler's tray in limed wood has hinged sides which fold down, turning it into a small oval table. It sits on an separate folding base and is ideal for impromptu meals indoors or in the garden.

This beech folding table is equally at home in modern or period decor. It features Classical S-shaped, or ogee, legs and dove-tailed joints. The pale wood mellows with prolonged exposure to daylight.

Scalloped jigsaw fretwork makes this little trestle table a bit out of the ordinary. Ideal for teas or light meals, it folds neatly and flatly away when not in use.

Eminently weatherproof and garden worthy, this teak folding table looks equally good indoors. The slatted wood surface is self draining after rain.

Featuring hand holes for ease of carrying, these Chinese red and decoupage-covered black jointed folding tables provide useful extra surface space.

BEDSIDE MANNERS

Bedside tables take up very little room but are quite indispensable in main and guest bedrooms alike. Small and compact, they're easy to improvise, so there's no reason why any bed should do without.

A bedside table is a must in any bedroom. It lets you keep a reading lamp, books and magazines, an alarm clock and a cup of steaming coffee at your fingertips as you recline against the pillows, as well as providing a display surface for a cherished photograph or a vase of fresh flowers. Small and compact, it's also a very easy piece of furniture to improvise, so there's no need to go without – even in spare bedrooms.

A quick glance around your home will reveal many items that can double up as bedside tables. A wicker hamper or wooden chest covered with a lacy topcloth will give an ample surface area, as well as useful storage space for bedlinen. Furniture borrowed from other rooms – an occasional table, a butler's tray, an upholstered footstool or even an elegant dining chair – can all be put to service by the bedside for the duration of a guest's stay.

Whichever item you choose, bear in mind that bedside tables should be roughly mattress height for the greatest ease of use. Pieces of furniture that are higher than this are awkward to reach.

A butler's tray does excellent service as a bedside table, where it carries books, an alarm clock, a candlelamp, a photograph and a vase of fresh flowers. Freed of some of its load, it would be just the thing for serving morning coffee in bed.

At its simplest, a bedside table may be no more than a pretty kitchen chair. Here, the rush seat provides a display surface for a pot brimming with freshly picked garden blooms as a bright welcome for a week-end guest.

Ever adaptable, a smart occasional table borrowed from the drawing room looks equally at home in a bedroom. A silky white cloth protects the surface and gives it a softer look. The table's lower shelf is ideal for storing books.

Maximize your storage space by using a sturdy wooden chest as a bedside table between twin beds. An exquisite lacy cloth provides a visual link with the bedlinen.

END OF THE BED

*Transform the empty space at the end of a bed
into a show place for a handsome storage chest, low-level
table or comfortable chair or sofa.*

Though bedside tables, bookcases and shelves next to or above a bedhead are common features, the space at the end of a bed is often wasted. In fact it is equally valuable, especially if the bedroom is small or the bed is viewed end on from the bedroom door.

A storage chest is a traditional end-of-bed feature and can double as a table for books, a bowl of pot pourri or vase of flowers. Bed-end chests are ideal for storing out-of-season clothes; as bottom drawers or hope chests they traditionally held a bride-to-be's trousseau and household linen. Covered with cushions, such a chest becomes an extra seat.

A comfortable chair, mini-sofa or chaise longue are also options, or a pair of occasional chairs and little table for the end of a king-sized bed. Upholstery and cushion covers can repeat or contrast with fabric used elsewhere in the room. The space at the end of a small child's bed also has potential – for a toy chest perhaps.

On a practical level, whatever you choose to position at the end of the bed, make sure there's adequate space to walk comfortably round it.

The natural tones and simple shape of this solid pine chest enhance the appearance of the bed and provide a table-like surface for storage or display. Beds with a simple frame or no frame especially benefit from the presence of furniture at their end.

▶ Where space allows, a generously large, well upholstered chaise longue makes a fitting focal point at the end of a king-sized bed. The cream fabric with royal blue spots perfectly complements the cream and blue colour scheme used throughout the bedroom.

▼ Elegant Regency curves in wrought iron comprise this bed frame and matching seat, upholstered in the same fabric as that used for the curtains, bedlinen and scatter cushions.

▲ Blanket coverage is on offer in this hand-painted pine blanket chest, complete with antique lock and handles. Alternatively, a plain chest can be stencilled or colourwashed to match the surrounding bedroom decor.

▶ Plain but pleasing, a chest made of dark-stained louvred panels provides a base for a photograph collection and the striking focal point for an all-white bedroom.

COMPACT DESKS

There are always occasions when a desk comes in handy, even if you're not running a business from home or have a student in the family. If space is limited, fold-up options are available, or you can just improvise.

For doing the ordinary day-to-day paperwork that's part of running a home or for writing personal letters, nothing beats a desk. But if space is at a premium, it may be hard to accommodate the bulk of a traditional desk; and if funds are limited the cost may be equally daunting. But with a bit of flair and imagination you can always improvise – adapt a fold-down table, for example, or fix a sturdy wall-hung, fold-down or fold-up panel to provide an instant writing surface.

First, find your spot, taking into account the other furniture in the room – you might want to face a window or know that you work better facing a wall. Unused alcoves are ideal. You'll need lighting, an electricity outlet and a telephone nearby.

Consider how the desk will look when not in use; and the appearance of any hinges, suspension chains or ropes – shiny brass fittings add class and outsized ropes give a touch of humour.

Choose an equally compact chair or stool that leaves space for your legs under the desk. Accessories can continue the streamlined theme, and might include wicker baskets suspended above the desk for files and other stationery. Or hang wall-hung terracotta half pots or wire hanging half baskets, sold for fixing to a garden wall, for storing your bits and pieces.

For a designer touch, you could paint the skirting boards and desk the same colour or hang a print or poster on the wall.

Leftover nooks such as this fireplace alcove are ideal for compact desks. Here, an improvised desktop, suspended from thick rope, and a colour coordinated tuck-under stool provide the basics; old wall-hung drainers keep necessities close at hand, or can even double up as plant or flower holders.

Virtually disappearing when not in use – note the painted hinges – this slightly sloping flap forms part of the fitted bookshelves which, in turn, are integrated into the architecture of the room.

As if by magic, a computer keyboard seems to float in space. In fact it rests on a narrow shelf fixed to the cupboard door, with the adjacent multi-level corner cupboard unit containing the screen, printer and other necessities.

Elegant and practical, this narrow drop-leaf table in black-stained pine is a mass-produced reproduction of an 18th century Swedish design. It provides a spacious work surface with one leaf up, but uses minimal space when the leaf is down.

Umbrella Stands

Umbrella stands are much more than simply useful storage items –
placed in the hallway, they provide a focal point and a display vehicle for
a handsome collection of walking sticks or umbrellas.

A place for everything and everything in its place is an essential motto for an orderly home – and placing an umbrella stand in your hallway is a step in the right direction. No more tripping over umbrellas and walking sticks propped untidily against walls, or hunting high and low for an umbrella when confronted with overcast skies just as you're dashing out of the door.

An umbrella stand is more than simply a practical storage item; choose an attractive style and it becomes a decorative accessory and welcome focal point in a hallway where there is usually little space for furniture and ornaments. You can turn it into a talking point by filling it with a collection of handsome wooden walking sticks or old-fashioned umbrellas with decoratively carved handles – keep an eye open for these in junk shops and antiques markets.

You'll find modern and traditional umbrella stands in metal, ceramic, wood or wicker. If you like, you can decorate them to suit their surroundings – with paint effects or decoupage, for example. Or if you're feeling creative, improvise a stand from a tall, wide-necked ceramic vase, a large metal ewer, a terracotta chimney pot or even a pair of well worn old boots, as shown above.

These boots were made for walking, but now they play a new role as a delightfully quirky umbrella stand. Make sure your umbrella is completely dry before you store it away in a non-waterproof stand like this one.

▶ An imploring dog, clasping his lead in his mouth, begs you to take him along as you remove your umbrella from his care and head out of the door.

▼ A wicker stand is an attractive, inexpensive option that suits most settings. Leave it natural, or spray paint it to complement the surrounding colour scheme.

▼ The height of chic, this blue and white ceramic umbrella stand is given a prime location in a reception room, where its handsome design and covetable contents can be admired at leisure.

▲ Be creative by painting and stencilling an old chimney pot to transform it into a smart and novel umbrella stand, which is sturdy enough to carry any number of sticks and umbrellas without toppling over.

ALL HOOKED UP

*That unrivalled home accessory, the unregarded coat-hook,
performs an important function, but with a little careful thought, a well placed
hook or two adds lively decorative detail to a room.*

You might not think of large flat expanses of wall or ceiling in terms of extra storage space. But simply adding a hook, or row of hooks, can turn an under-used area into a hardworking one. That is only part of the story, however. With a wide range of hooks available for a variety of purposes, the hooks and what you hang on them should be a positive addition to your decor. Get it wrong and you may end up with an untidy mess cluttering the clean lines of your room. But with care and planning you can add islands of interest to otherwise plain and boring walls.

Don't ignore the merits of the traditional row of metal coat-hooks. With a boldly coloured fascia board, it provides a focal point in a hallway. But there is more to hooks than a twist of chromed steel. Colourful metal cutouts of animals or fruit, with the hook as an incidental, are attractive in their own right. Wooden peg rails, painted Shaker colours, bring order to a room, and shelves with a row of hooks underneath perform a dual storage role.

But no matter how lovely the hooks you've chosen, the decorative effects are spoiled by clutter. Get the right size of hook for the objects you want to hang, and remember not to overload the hooks.

Painted to match the rest of the woodwork, this peg rail is a feature not an eyesore. It's not only useful, but the coats hats add a welcome splash of colour. But keep it simple. The same peg rail, overloaded with jackets, coats, hats and caps would make the entire hall look cluttered.

▼ Stencilled vine leaves *customize a plain wooden shelf set with a double row of useful peg hooks on which to hang culinary implements. Plain wooden peg rail shelves are available as kits from many do-it-yourself stores.*

▲ A row of stars, *stamped out from weather-beaten copper, makes a quaint and decorative heading for this row of hooks. What better place to hang your recycling bags?*

▼ Hearts made from twists *of wire provide a humorous way of supporting appliquéd pot holders so they're close to hand in a kitchen. The heart motif of the wire hooks repeats the whimsical theme of the appliqué motifs.*

▲ Fruit, vegetables and animals *are regular themes for decorative, painted metal hooks. They make a lively and appropriate choice for a kitchen.*

CLOTHES STORAGE

Hanging fabric covers are a practical way to keep clothes clean and tidy, whether they're in daily use or in seasonal storage. If you're short on space, consider making some hanging fabric shelves, too.

F inding enough wardrobe storage space for all the family's clothes can be a problem. Open rails and peg racks provide an excellent and cost-effective solution, yet clothes left out for any length of time become dusty and are likely to look untidy. Fabric covers are an ideal way to create a sense of order, as well as keeping the clothes crease and dust-free.

You can make the covers in fabrics to match your other soft furnishings, or colour code them according to their contents – the options are varied. Natural fabrics such as cotton and linen are the best choice for making the covers,

as unlike plastic and other non-porous materials they allow the air to circulate around the clothes, keeping them fresh and aired. You can also match the covers with linking accessories, such as padded coat hangers and lavender-scented sachets which keep moths at bay.

Hanging shelves are another practical storage solution. Made from fabric reinforced with thin plywood, the shelves are hung from an open rail or inside a roomy wardrobe to give additional storage for items that you can fold away, such as knitwear, or accessories that are awkward to store, like handbags and shoes.

Fabric clothes covers and hanging fabric shelves really come into their own where storage space is limited. Here, made to match their surroundings, they slot in neatly and inconspicuously on a hanging rail amongst the drawers of an open storage unit.

MAKING A CLOTHES COVER

These instructions are for a clothes cover which measures 55cm (20½in) wide and 90cm (35½in) long from the neck opening to the turn-up fold. This is long enough to house most separates. If you want to make a longer cover – for a dress, for example – put the garment on the hanger and measure from the hanger neck to the garment hem; add 5cm (2in) 'breathing space' plus 25cm (9½in) for the buttoned turn-up.

For 120cm (47½in) wide fabric, cut the cover from across the fabric width. For narrower widths, allow extra fabric, and cut out the cover along the fabric length. A 6mm (¼in) seam allowance is included in the pattern.

YOU WILL NEED

❖ STURDY COAT HANGER

❖ DRESSMAKERS' PATTERN PAPER

❖ DRESSMAKERS' MARKER PEN AND RULER

❖ 120cm (1⅜yd) of 120cm (47½in) WIDE FABRIC

❖ 4m (4⅜yd) BIAS BINDING, 1.5cm (⅝in) finished width

❖ FOUR BUTTONS, 2cm (¾in) in diameter

❖ MATCHING SEWING THREAD

❖ TWO PRESS-STUDS (optional)

1 **Transferring the pattern** Fold a large piece of pattern paper in half. Scale up the half-pattern on to the folded piece of pattern paper, with the dotted pattern line lying along the fold; adjust the length and angle of the shoulder slope if necessary to follow the shape of your coat hanger. Carefully cut along the solid pattern lines. Open out the pattern.

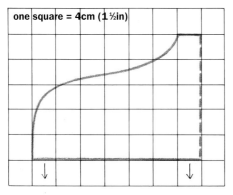

one square = 4cm (1½in)

2 **Cutting out the cover** Fold and pin the fabric double, with the fold on the straight grain. Pin the pattern in place. To extend the pattern length, use a ruler and marker pen to measure and mark the fabric 95cm (37½in) below the base edge of the pattern on each side. Cut out the two cover pieces.

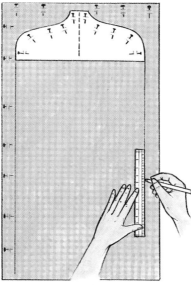

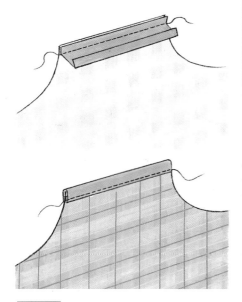

3 **Binding the top openings** Cut two 8cm (3in) lengths of bias binding. Lay one length along the neck opening of one cover piece, with the right side of the binding facing the wrong side of the cover piece and matching the edges. Stitch in place along the binding fold line, 6mm (¼in) from the fabric edge. Fold the binding to the right side and machine stitch in place through all layers. Repeat for the other piece.

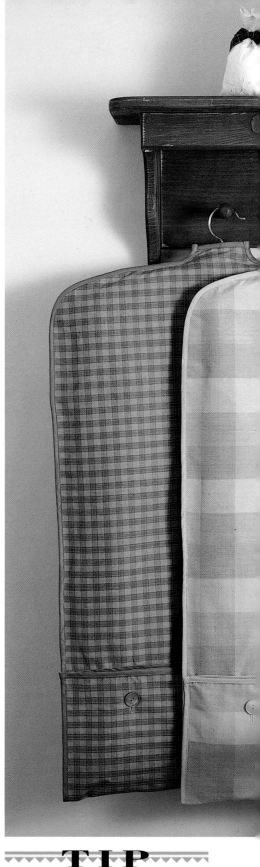

TIP

SHAPED TO FIT

You can adapt the pattern given here to fit any shape of hanger. Simply align the hanging hook with the pattern centre, then draw the outline of the hanger on to the pattern. Adjust the length or slope of the shoulder seam as necessary, then cut out the pattern.

Coordinating clothes covers and matching padded hangers in crisp checked fabrics, neatly trimmed with binding and buttons, are a smart way to keep clothes clean and your storage space tidy.

4 Binding the base Neaten the base edge of each cover piece using machine zigzag stitch, then fold over 5cm (2in) to the wrong side and press – this turning supports the buttonholes. Cut two 56cm (21in) lengths of bias binding. Starting on the wrong side, stitch one length in place along the folded base edge of each cover piece, as in step 3.

5 Joining the cover pieces Place the cover pieces together with wrong sides facing. Starting at the coat hanger opening and taking a 6mm (¼in) seam allowance, machine stitch down each side. Stitch binding along each side to cover the previous stitching lines, as in step 3, tucking in the ends to neaten.

6 Adding buttonholes Measure 2.5cm (1in) above the bound base edges on both the front and back section of the cover. At this level, measure and mark a vertical buttonhole 11cm (4⅛in) in from each side of the cover, on both sections. Measure and mark two more buttonholes in-between, about 11cm (4⅛in) apart, on both sections. Machine stitch all the buttonholes – eight in total.

7 Finishing off Fold up the base edges by 20cm (7½in). Reaching through both sets of buttonholes, use a dressmakers' pencil to mark the position for the four buttons on the cover. Stitch the buttons in place, making sure you create button shanks long enough to accommodate the fabric thicknesses. Insert the coat hanger through the base opening. If you find the side edges of the buttoned turn-up sag, you can secure them with a press-stud at each end.

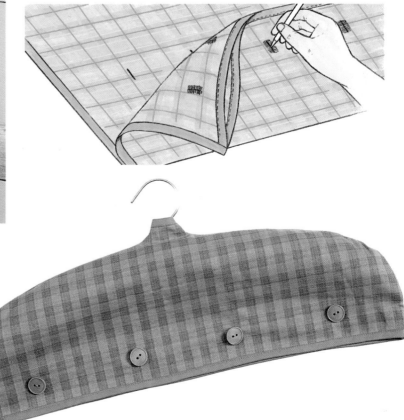

Padded, fabric-covered coat hangers help keep garments in shape, so are a sensible addition to a wardrobe. This cover is made in a similar way to the clothes covers, except that the hem edge is not folded up. Before covering the hanger, pad it by winding strips of wadding around it, securing the ends with a few stitches.

FABRIC SHELVES

Increase your storage space with fabric hanging shelves – they are great for stacking away shoes or folded sweaters. The completed shelves measure 24cm (9½in) wide by 110cm (45in) high by 32cm (12½in) deep. Take 1cm (⅜in) seams throughout.

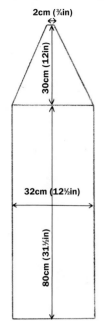

2cm (¾in)

30cm (12in)

32cm (12½in)

80cm (31½in)

YOU WILL NEED

- ❖ PENCIL AND RULER
- ❖ PATTERN PAPER OR NEWSPAPER
- ❖ SCISSORS
- ❖ 1.9m (2¼yd) of FURNISHING FABRIC, 150cm (60in) wide
- ❖ D-RING 2.5cm (1in)
- ❖ VELCRO
- ❖ THIN PLYWOOD, five 270 x 310mm (10¾ x 12¼in) rectangles

▶ *Natural cotton fabrics in restful neutral shades make up into highly versatile hanging storage, which fits in with most schemes.*

1 Using the pattern On paper, enlarge the *side panel pattern* above to the correct size and cut it out. Fold the fabric double and pin the pattern on to it. Cut around it, adding 1cm (⅜in) all round for seams. Unpin the pattern. Use the triangular pattern piece to cut out two triangular facings in the same way, adding 1cm (⅜in) all round.

2 Cutting out the remaining pieces *For the shelf coverings* cut out five 30 x 66cm (12 x 26in) rectangles. *For the side facings* cut out eight 22 x 34cm (8¾in x 13½in) rectangles. *For the hanging loop* cut a 5cm (2in) square.

3 Preparing the shelf coverings On the short ends of each shelf covering, press a 1cm (⅜in) turning to the wrong side. With the right side out, press each shelf covering in half, so the pressed seams align. These sit at the back of the shelves and are left open to insert the plywood boards.

4 Joining the top facings Position the two triangular facings on each side of one folded shelf covering, raw edges matching. Position two side facings underneath the folded shelf covering. The side facings and triangles extend 1cm (⅜in) beyond the front and back edges of the shelf covering to allow for seams later. Pin and stitch through all layers.

5 Joining in the remaining shelves Follow step 4 to join the lower edge of the already assembled side facings to the remaining shelf covers and side facings. Sandwich the shelf covers between the side facings in each case. Press each section as it is stitched. At the last shelf, press the turnings up.

6 Facing the shelves With right sides together and assembled shelves folded up in-between, pin, tack then stitch one side panel piece to the front and back edges of one side of the shelves. Trim the seam allowance at the corners and turn to the right side. Repeat with the remaining side panel.

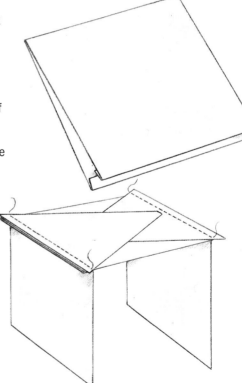

7 Finishing the cover Slipstitch the base edge of the outside panels to the lower shelf. Insert the plywood pieces and slipstitch the openings closed.

8 Stitching the loop Right sides facing, fold the loop fabric square in half and stitch a 6mm (¼in) seam. Turn and fold the strip over the D-ring. Stitch just under the ring. Sandwich the ends of the loop between the triangle tops and stitch.

TENTED WARDROBES

*Free-standing fabric wardrobes are a perfect solution when storage space
is at a premium. Start with a special kit or re-cover a shop-bought wardrobe to
create a striking, themed accessory to complement your decor.*

F abric tented wardrobes are great for absorbing the overspill from conventional wardrobes, or for providing budget-conscious and decorative hanging storage in a guest room or studio flat. They're an especially popular choice for children's rooms where, covered with jazzy checks, spots or nursery prints, they help create a fun, stimulating environment, as well as doubling unofficially as play tents.

Tented wardrobes are available from large department and home stores or by mail order in two basic styles – with a flat or a sloping top. Some styles are sold with a cover included, but if you want to give your wardrobe a special twist, making a new cover is straightforward and needn't be expensive.

Take inspiration from the shape of the wardrobe – those with sloping tops conjure up a delightful beach hut image, which you can emphasize with a cover in wide ice-cream coloured stripes and sturdy natural fabrics such as ticking, calico or sandwashed denim. Or you could use stripes in stronger colours, such as red, blue and white, to create a smart, military campaign-tent look. A wardrobe dressed with toile de Jouy or a flowery chintz cover trimmed with rosettes or bows has romantic, fairytale appeal; or for a theatrical flourish, choose exotic, richly coloured fabrics and embellish these with cords, fringes and tassels. Finish your wardrobe cover with a valance trim, shaped to complement its decorative style.

This tented wardrobe is covered in a creative combination of checks and an alphabetical print, to coordinate perfectly with its surroundings. The unusual valance is formed from a double layer of zigzagging pennants.

MAKING A FITTED COVER

These instructions show how to make a cover for a free-standing, flat-topped wardrobe, like the one shown opposite. The cover featured here has a decorative scallop-shaped valance, and bow ties to secure the front opening flaps. To ensure that the scallops lie evenly across the front, and at the front corners and sides on any size of free-standing wardrobe, the valance is shaped on three sides only, and left straight at the back. The fabric amounts given here are for a wardrobe measuring 167cm (65¾in) high, 82cm (32¼in) wide and 51cm (20in) deep. If your wardrobe is a different size, measure for the patterns in the same way as here, and allow for more or less fabric as appropriate.

YOU WILL NEED

- ❖ FREE-STANDING WARDROBE FRAME with flat top
- ❖ NEWSPAPER AND STICKY TAPE
- ❖ TAPE MEASURE
- ❖ RULER, PENCIL AND PAIR OF COMPASSES
- ❖ SCISSORS
- ❖ 5.5m (6yd) FABRIC, 140cm (54in) wide
- ❖ MEDIUMWEIGHT IRON-ON INTERFACING, 2.5m (2¾yd)
- ❖ MATCHING THREAD

MAKING THE PATTERN PIECES

Before you begin measuring up, erect the wardrobe frame and join sheets of newspaper with sticky tape to create panels large enough to fit each separate section of the wardrobe frame. If your wardrobe already has a cover, you can use this as your pattern guide. Remember to allow extra for the valance when purchasing the fabric. The pattern sizes given here allow for 1.5cm (⅝in) seam allowances and a 5cm (2in) base hem.

1 Making the main patterns Draw each of the following on to paper:
For the back: Measure the wardrobe height (**A**) and its width (**B**). Add 7.5cm (3in) to **A** and 3cm (1¼in) to **B**, and draw a rectangle to this size.
For the front pieces: Add 7.5cm (3in) to **A**. Halve **B**'s width and add 14.5cm (5¾in) to this sum to allow for a facing on the front leading edge, and a seam allowance at the opposite edge. Mark up this size.
For the sides: Measure the wardrobe depth (**C**). Add 7.5cm (3in) to **A** and 3cm (1¼in) to **C**. Mark up this size.
For the top: Add 3cm (1¼in) to **B** and the same to **C**. Mark up this size.

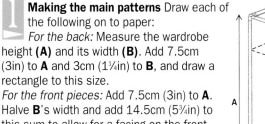

2 Making valance patterns
For the front and back: Decide on the depth of the valance, including seam allowances (**V**) – usually about 18cm (7in). Draw two rectangles **B** x **V**. Add on and mark a 1.5cm (⅝in) seam allowance at both short ends of each rectangle.
For the valance sides: Draw a rectangle **C** x **V**. Add the side seam allowances as for the valance front.

3 Shaping the front valance Fold one valance front pattern in half widthways. Starting at the centre, use a ruler and pencil to divide the length to the marked seam allowance into four equal sections. Mark the depth of the scallops as a line across the pattern. Use a pair of compasses to draw the scallops, and cut out 1.5cm (⅝in) below the curves. Open out the pattern.

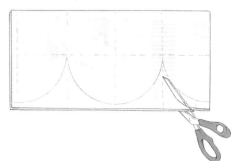

◤ *You can soften the lines of a functional, flat-topped tented wardrobe by making a cover with a deep scalloped valance and full bow ties at the leading edges.*

4 Shaping the side valance Lay the shaped valance front pattern over the valance side pattern, lining them up at one short end. Draw round to mark as many scallops and part-scallops as will fit on to the side pattern. Cut along the marked lines.

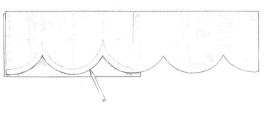

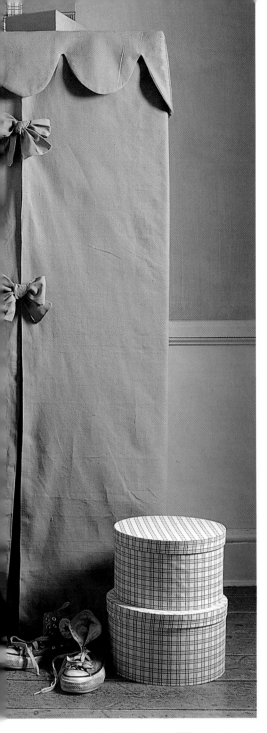

STITCHING THE COVER

1 **Cutting out** Use the patterns to cut out the following:
From main fabric: For the main cover, cut one back, two fronts, two sides and one top piece. For the valance, cut two front pieces using the shaped front pattern, and two backs using the unshaped back pattern; also cut four shaped side pieces. For the ties, cut four 35 x 8cm (13¾ x 3¼in) strips.
From interfacing: For the main cover front facings, cut two **A** x 13cm (5⅛in) lengths. For the valance, cut one unshaped back piece, one shaped front piece and two shaped sides.

2 **Making the valance** Fuse the valance interfacing pieces to the wrong side of corresponding fabric pieces. Right sides together, pin, tack and stitch the interfaced valance pieces together, end to end in the right order. Press seams open. Repeat for the remaining valance pieces (the facings), then turn right side out. With right sides together and seams aligned, match the valance bands and stitch around the curves. Clip round the curves, turn right side out and press.

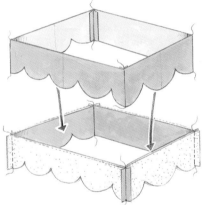

3 **Adding the top panel** With right sides together and raw edges level, lay the valance over the top panel, aligning all corner seams with the top panel corners. Pin and stitch the layers together, opening the valance seams slightly to ease the fit if necessary.

4 **Stitching the fronts** On each main cover front piece, turn 13cm (5⅛in) on the leading edge to the wrong side and press to mark the facings. Open out again, then fuse interfacing strips to the wrong side of each leading edge. Turn in and stitch a 6mm (¼in) hem through all thicknesses. Refold each facing along the pressed line, and stitch the top edges together to secure. Align the leading edges and secure with a few stitches through all thicknesses at the top edge.

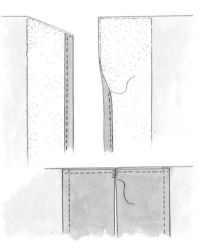

5 **Making up the panels** With right sides together, pin, tack and stitch a side panel to each side of a front panel. Then join the other side of each side panel to the back panel. Neaten the seam edges and press the seams open.

6 **Assembling the wardrobe** Turn the wardrobe panels wrong side out. With right sides together, slip the valance into the top of the wardrobe panels, matching the raw edges and aligning the corner seams. Stitch together through all thicknesses. Neaten the seams and turn right side out.

7 **Finishing off** Fit the cover over the wardrobe frame and check the fit. Pin the hem. To make the ties, fold each strip in half along its length, right sides together. Stitch, taking a 1.5cm (⅝in) seam, turn out and press. Tuck in the short ends and slipstitch closed. Pin the ties, positioning them as desired, to the wrong side of the front leading edges. Remove the cover. Stitch the ties in place. Turn under a 6mm (¼in) hem on the base edge and machine stitch, then turn up to the desired length and machine or hand stitch in place.

◆ ◆ ◆ ◆ T I P ◆ ◆ ◆ ◆

TENTED WARDROBE LININGS

For a luxurious effect, make a lining for your tented wardrobe from contrasting plain or patterned fabric.

Simply cut out the basic pattern pieces twice, but for the linings omit the front panel facings and the valance. Join the lining sections together, then fit the lining right side down over the wardrobe frame, before the main cover. You can anchor the lining to the main cover at the front opening with poppers or touch-and-close fastening spots (Velcro).

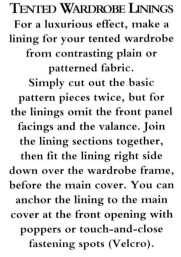

Some tented wardrobes have such steeply sloping tops, that you need to make the top section from four fabric pieces rather than one. The rest of the cover is made up in the same way as for the flat-topped version.

1 Making the patterns Make all patterns, except the top pattern, as for *Making a Fitted Cover*.

For the sloping roof sides: Measure one rectangular, sloping side of the wardrobe top, from the summit to the base **(A)**, and add 3cm (1¼in). Measure the width of the same side **(B)**, and add 3cm (1¼in). Cut a paper rectangle to this size.

For the vertical roof sides: Measure across the base edge of one triangular, vertical side of the roof **(C)**. Measure from the centre of the base edge to the highest point of the triangle **(D)**. Draw a triangle to this size on paper, then mark a line 1.5cm (⅝in) outside all round. Cut out along the outer line.

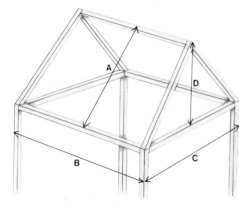

2 Stitching the tent top Use the roof patterns to cut two rectangles and two triangles from fabric. With right sides together and raw edges level, pin, tack and stitch the two rectangles together along the top edge. Press the seam open. With right sides together and raw edges level, fit a triangle to one end of the rectangles. Stitch in place, pivoting the needle at the central top seam. Repeat for the other triangle.

3 Making up the cover Make up the cover exactly as for *Making a Fitted Cover, Stitching the Cover*, attaching the shaped top piece as for the flat one, matching corner seams. Omit or reposition the front ties as appropriate.

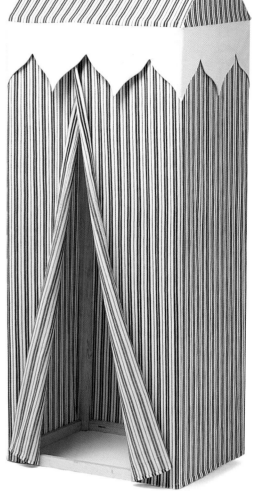

▲ *Give a sloping tented wardrobe a smart, campaign-style feel with a navy, black and cream striped cover and cream, petal-shaped valance.*

DIFFERENT VALANCE SHAPES

You can adapt the valance shape on your tented wardrobe to suit the mood of the decor, using petals or pennants as shown below. The petals are a pretty variation on the curved scallop shape, while the pennants are simply formed using a ruler in a straightforward zigzag design.

Making a petal pattern Prepare the front valance pattern piece as for *Making a Fitted Cover, Making the Pattern Pieces* step 2, but make the valance slightly deeper to accommodate the petal tips. Fold the pattern in half widthways, and divide the space from the fold to the seam allowance into an odd number of equal width sections. Starting at the fold with a whole scallop, use a pair of compasses to mark scallops across the paper. Extend the base edges of each scallop to form a petal point, as shown. Cut out 1.5cm (⅝in) below the petal outlines. Trace the shaped edge on to the valance side patterns as *Making the Pattern Pieces* step 4.

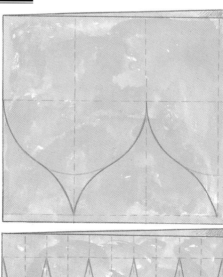

Making a pennant pattern Prepare the front valance pattern piece as for *Making a Fitted Cover, Making the Pattern Pieces* step 2, but make the valance slightly deeper if desired. Fold the pattern in half widthways, and divide the space from the fold to the seam allowance into an even number of equal width sections, each one to represent one half of a pennant. Starting at the fold with a whole pennant, use a ruler to draw in the pennant shapes to the desired depth, as shown. Cut out 1.5cm (⅝in) beyond the pennant outlines. Trace the shaped edge on to the valance side pattern pieces.

Children's Storage

Easy-to-reach, sturdy storage units or containers in bold, simple shapes and colours, with easily managed lids, encourage tidiness and give character to a child's room.

G etting young children to keep their rooms in order can be a challenging parental task but if you provide plenty of imaginative storage units or containers that are fun to use, or even double as toys themselves, you're halfway there.

Try to coordinate the units with the colour, scale and style of the existing decor, ensuring that they are large enough to do their job without too much loss of floor space for play. Children like to be involved in making the choice – even by just picking the colour, they feel more like a proud owner and respond accordingly. Encouraging them to help decide which items go where also makes for a sense of ownership.

A combination of fitted and movable units is ideal and flexible enough to respond to a growing child's changing interests, needs and possessions. If some smaller movable units fit neatly into the fitted units, so much the better. Modular units are easily adjustable and expandable, and are especially appropriate for a small room where a collection of various storage units is in danger of adding to the clutter. In a small room, consider stacking units, and don't forget potential storage space under the bed or cot.

Try to add a personal touch such as a monogram or stick-on pictures of children's favourite cartoon character or television star, or stencilled motifs to match those on furniture, floor or walls. Finally, safety is an important factor: make sure units or containers are stable, screw freestanding shelves to the wall, and avoid sharp edges and lids that can trap small fingers.

Boldly striped in primary colours to match the room, this user-friendly trio of large wooden storage boxes takes the form of a friendly bear, alligator and spotted dog. Once the animal motifs are outgrown, the heads and feet can be removed.

◀ All aboard! It's hard for a young child to resist filling these colourful carriages – with storage as fun as this, clearing up will quickly become a natural extension of playing.

▼ Movable storage units can be geared to the specific age and whims of a child but more costly fitted storage units that are basically neutral remain useful from infancy through to adolescence. Their ever-changing contents can reflect the child's developing interests.

▼ Wooden pegs in an expandable diamond pattern add strong graphic interest to this wall, and provide hanging space for colourful storage bags.

▲ A classic car wall hook adds a flashy modern touch to a young child's bedroom; a collection of several different models displayed in rows can form a handsome focal point.

LADDER STORAGE

Clear the decks of clutter with a wooden, ladder-style storage rack. Simple to make from a few lengths of timber, a ladder rack is a quick, inexpensive and convenient solution for holding items in frequent use.

A ladder storage rack, mounted on the wall above your kitchen counter, hobby table or desktop, is ideal for storing items in regular use, allowing you to keep the work surface clear while still having everything within easy reach. With the addition of a few butchers' hooks you can hang items from the ladder rungs, use large bulldog clips to fasten messages, recipes and pictures, or tie on baskets to house smaller odds and ends.

All the pieces of the pine storage rack described overleaf are made from the same size timber which is simply cut to length, sanded smooth and assembled in a ladder shape – horizontal rungs fixed between two vertical uprights. To suit a bathroom or kitchen environment, the rack is sealed with a coat of clear polyurethane spray.

In the kitchen, a rack positioned close to a work surface is ideal for hanging pots and pans, graters, sieves and spoons that are rarely out of service. You can also take the opportunity to display attractive items, such as polished brass pans, freeing cupboard space for other items. Or you can use the rack purely as a decorative feature – decked with old-fashioned kitchenware, interesting shaped pastry cutters, bunches of dried herbs and colourful spices such as crimson chillies.

In other rooms in the home, there are plenty of ways to put your rack to good use – as a bathroom towel rail or office organizer, for example. Different storage ideas and ways to adapt the rail to fit your exact requirements or decorative frame are described on the following pages.

Ladder storage can be adapted to suit the items you need to store. Here, sawn timber painted blue is made into a trellis work of uprights and rungs, forming a handy pan lid and knife rack. Dowels form the rungs of a separate ladder with butchers' hooks used to hang pans and other kitchen accessories.

MAKING A LADDER RACK

You can adjust the dimensions so that your ladder rack fits a particular space, or is large enough to hold a number of items. The pine rack shown here measures 76 x 40cm (30 x 15¾in) and requires about 5.4m (18ft) of planed timber. Allowing a little extra for mistakes, you need to buy two lengths of timber measuring 2.7 and 3m (9 and 10ft).

For a ladder rack measuring more than about 91cm (3ft) wide, from which you will hang heavy items, it's a wise precaution to fix an extra central upright for stronger support.

When buying the wood, look for lengths with a straight, even grain that's free from knots – these may look attractive but could cause the wood to warp or crack.

For quicker results you may be able to have all the timber lengths cut to size at a timber merchant or DIY store. Pine is one of the easiest timbers to work with.

1 Cutting the uprights Measure and mark two 760mm (30in) lengths of timber. Use a try square to carry the marks round the sides of the wood. On the back face of each piece, score along the cutting line with a craft knife to prevent splintering when sawing through. Cut the wood to length with a tenon saw and sand the edges smooth.

2 Cutting the rungs Measure and mark nine 400mm (15¾in) lengths of planed timber, carrying the measurements around the sides and scoring the back as before. Cut the lengths and sand smooth.

3 Rounding off the rungs (optional) Round off the top and facing edges of each rung with coarse abrasive paper. Or for a professional finish, set a marking gauge to 4mm (⁵⁄₃₂in) and run it along the top and facing edges of each rung. Secure the rungs in a workbench and plane at an angle along the top edges, down to the scored lines. Sand smooth.

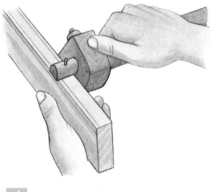

4 Marking the uprights Set a marking gauge to half the width of the upright and run it along the length of each uprights' back face. Or use a pencil and straightedge to mark along the middle of the back face. On each upright, measure 40mm (1½in) down from the top edge and mark this point on the middle line. Continue down the uprights, marking points at 85mm (3⅜in) intervals and stopping 40mm (1½in) from the bottom edge.

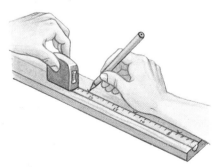

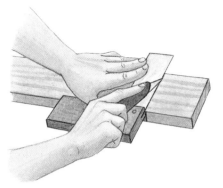

5 Drilling the uprights Drill a 4mm (⁵⁄₃₂in) clearance hole at each mark on the back of the uprights, turning the wood over to finish drilling from the front to prevent splintering. Countersink the holes from the back.

6 Drilling the rungs On the back of each rung, measure 60mm (1¼in) from each end and mark a point halfway across the width. Using a 2mm (³⁄₃₂in) bit and depth stop, drill a 6mm (¼in) deep pilot hole at each mark.

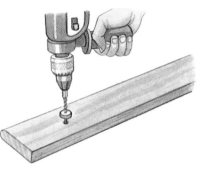

7 Fixing the rungs Working on one rung at a time, apply adhesive around the screw holes, then loosely screw the rungs to the front face of the uprights, using 25mm (1in) No 8 countersunk screws. As you work, use a try square to check the rungs and uprights are square, then tighten all the screws and wipe off any smears of adhesive.

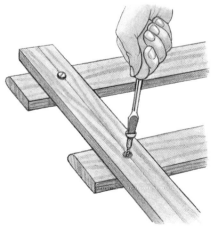

Making the fixing holes
Lay the rack face down and mark a point on the scored line of both uprights, halfway between the top two rungs. Start drilling a 4mm ($\frac{5}{32}$in) hole at the mark, stopping when the point of the bit starts to come through the other side, then turn the rack over and finish drilling from the other side.

Finishing the ladder If painting, fill any gaps with wood filler. Sand all the surfaces smooth then spray with two coats of clear matt polyurethane varnish or apply wood primer and paint. Allow to dry. Hold the rack in position on the wall using a spirit level to check it is level.

Fixing the ladder Transfer the screw hole positions on to the wall and use a drill and masonry bit to drill holes at the marks. Insert wallplugs. Thread brass screw cups on to 50mm (2in) brass No 8 countersunk screws and screw the rack to the wall.

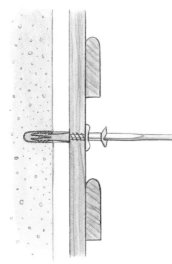

▷ *The basic styling of this wooden ladder rack blends with a range of decorative looks, from the sleek lines of a modern brushed steel kitchen to the rustic look of the unfitted kitchen.*

LADDER IDEAS

Ladder storage racks can be made in all shapes and sizes and used throughout the home. Depending on where and how you want to use your ladder rack you can customize it to exact specifications – change the dimensions to fit a certain space; adjust the rung spacing to accommodate particular items; and add extra fixings such as coat hooks.

If you want to make an unusual shaped ladder, with a circular, triangular or fish-shaped outline for example, start off by making a scale drawing of the shape and marking on the positions of the uprights and rungs. Enlarge the drawing to the desired size and cut the wood to match – cutting the rungs and uprights to different lengths; angling or curving the ends of the wood, or placing the uprights at an angle as appropriate.

Laid horizontally, there are even more ways to put your rack to good use. Made to the same dimensions but without the wall fixings, you can use the rack as a duck-board style bath mat – then make a miniature version as a soap drainer. Smaller models, strengthened with an extra upright batten, also make good serving mats on which to stand hot pans and dishes.

☑ *Ladder rungs provide useful staging posts for wire baskets holding desktop bits and pieces. At a desk or hobby table, fix the ladder in front of your chair position so the items are within reach.*

Made to measure Make the most of available space – in an alcove or across a chimney breast, for example – by adapting the dimensions of the rack to fit.

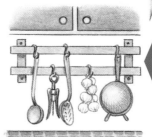

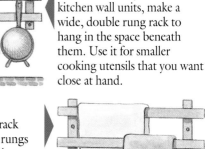

Under units If you have kitchen wall units, make a wide, double rung rack to hang in the space beneath them. Use it for smaller cooking utensils that you want close at hand.

Towel rail In the bathroom, make a rack with widely spaced rungs for towels. Use thicker wood for the uprights, so the rungs are further from the wall, allowing more space for fluffy towels.

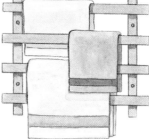

Coat rack Screw coat hooks to some of the rungs and use the ladder for all your outdoor paraphernalia – hats, coats, scarfs and umbrellas.

Tie rack Make a miniature ladder with a hook fixing at the top and hang in your wardrobe as a tie rack.

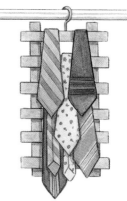

Noticeboard Add some outsize bulldog clips and use the ladder as a study noticeboard or a display space for your children's paintings.

Duck board For a complete rethink, why not lay the storage idea to rest, omit the wall fixings and use your rack as a duck-board bath mat?

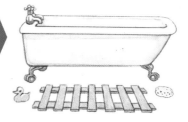

PLATE RACKS

Providing practical storage and constructed from natural materials, wooden plate racks have quietly proved their worth, generation after generation.

A high-tech kitchen, full of the latest gadgets, utensils and appliances, certainly has its advantages, but there's something immensely reassuring about an old-fashioned wooden plate rack. In terms of design, its form follows its function absolutely. The simplest types consist of a series of parallel vertical dowels providing the support for a single row of plates. Larger racks have two or more tiers, often of different sizes to accommodate smaller plates and other utensils. Some may have elaborately fretted pelmets – the Victorians loved fretwork – further embellished with hand-painted motifs.

Unlike plastic-coated metal plate racks, which tend to crack and rust after a few years, wooden plate racks are virtually indestructible. Look for them in junk shops, secondhand shops or, at the other end of the market, antique shops and stylish kitchen stores. If you buy a secondhand plate rack, wash it thoroughly.

Hang plate racks according to intended use – over the draining board and within easy reach of the sink if used for drying plates; out of the way for storing little-used plates. Screw the rack to the wall using mirror plates or directly through the wood. Before fixing, have someone hold it in position to test whether the height is convenient, and test its strength afterwards before filling with plates. Depending on the design, plate racks can also be free standing.

Shaker-like purity of design ensures that the simplest wooden plate racks look appropriate in kitchens ranging from country-cottage and Victorian to Colonial American and modern apartment style.

◀ Elegant metal brackets help support this multi-tiered, stained wood plate rack. With a variety of shelves and hooks, there's plenty of room for storing garlic ropes as well as cups, mugs and plates.

▶ With its intricate arches, this elaborate plate rack-cum-shelf is impressive enough to merit a place in the dining room or parlour. The central, stage-like shelves are ideal for displaying a collection of antique china.

▲ Hand painted in subtle shades of dusky pink and slate grey, including horizontal pink stripes across the dowels and stencilled circles, this handsome plate rack incorporates a towel rail and shelf for multiple storage.

STORING WINE

*By storing wine correctly you can retain and enhance
its quality – and by storing wine attractively you can enjoy
watching your collection grow.*

Wines are not only fun to drink but also to collect and learn about – many supermarkets and wine merchants display helpful signs, describing the variety of grape, area of origin, taste, degree of sweetness and serving suggestions for each wine. With shops and newspapers regularly running special offers, and with the opportunity to bring back duty-free from abroad, it often pays to buy in bulk. So if you have more than a few bottles you'll need somewhere to store them.

If you're serious about large-scale collection and top quality wines, an underground cellar or dark room kept at an even 10-13°C (50-55°F) is ideal – a bit of dampness causes no real harm though labels may become unstuck, but garages and outhouses that are vulnerable to frost are unsuitable. Alternatively, for the serious connoisseur some wine merchants store wine for an annual fee.

For just a few bottles, however, with a quick turnover between shop and consumption, a rack in the dining room or kitchen is fine, provided it is well away from central heating and bright light, which fades colour and causes taste to deteriorate.

You can buy rigid or extendible freestanding racks or convert a cupboard or other piece of furniture. Some fitted units offer optional, built-in wine racks. Low-level storage is generally better than high since heat rises. Always store wine horizontally to stop the cork drying out and cracking, which lets air in and makes the wine become corked.

Shaker-like in its simplicity, this sturdy wooden wine rack features vertical planks with semi-circular cut-outs in which the bottle necks rest. The recessed shelves and planks help protect the wine from exposure to light – essential for medium- or long-term storage.

◀ *Elegant wirework* tracery racks can house mineral water or a selection of flavoured cooking oils, as well as wine. They are a stylish accessory for a kitchen or dining room.

◣ *Improvising can be fun*, and this disused cooking range makes an unusual wine store, though piling bottles one on another demands slow and careful extraction.

◀ *Slightly tilting bottles* neck down ensures that no air occurs between wine and cork. This rustic, freestanding rack would be equally practical in a hall or spare bedroom.

◣ *Cheap, lightweight and portable,* this little bamboo wine rack is ideal for just a few bottles. For instant identification without having to disturb the bottles, always place wines with their labels uppermost.

SMALL CUPBOARDS

*Every home needs more cupboard space.
Small cupboards hung on the wall provide practical
storage with style.*

In hard-working areas of the home, such as kitchens and bathrooms, places to put things can be in short supply. When the items in question are small and might be easily overlooked in drawers or shelves, the answer is to keep them neat and tidy in a wall cupboard hung conveniently at eye level.

With a little imagination, these simple cupboards can become attractive features in their own right. A splash of colour and an eye for arrangement can transform even the humblest junk shop buy into a focus for decorative display. Try hand-painting special motifs on the doors or sides for an individual look, or display favourite ornaments in cupboards with no doors.

Small wooden cupboards are not difficult to construct. If you have some basic woodworking skills, you could make your own from solid wood, MDF (medium density fibreboard) or tongue-and-groove panelling. Otherwise, you can revamp old cupboards discovered in junk shops or antique markets using simple decorative techniques. There's no need to worry about fine finishes – a rustic country-style effect can be very charming.

Positioning is important. Hang the cupboard in a convenient place within easy reach. Two or more cupboards hung together in a group increase the impact. As a frame for display or a means of hiding clutter from view, the small cupboard more than earns its keep.

Decorative shaping adds interest to a plain cupboard, echoing the curvy shelf edging below. Such effects are easy to achieve in MDF. The strong matt shades of green and pink enliven the effect.

▲ **Simply constructed,** this wooden framework makes a decorative housing for a wall-mounted phone, with a drawer for notepaper and addresses neatly integrated underneath.

▼ **Searing egg-yolk yellow** unites a wall-hung arrangement of different cupboards. A letter rack mounted on the wall is the perfect place to keep memos.

▶ **With its doors removed,** the interior of this cupboard can be used as open shelving for arranging eye-catching objects, while the top of the cupboard provides a surface for propping up pictures.

HANDMADE BOXES

*Although simple storage furniture in flatpack or ready-made form
can be relatively inexpensive, the challenge and satisfaction of making an entire
small piece of furniture by hand is hard to beat.*

A simple wooden box or cupboard makes a fun and very practical starting point for putting some basic woodworking skills into practice. These small pieces of furniture are tough and durable, and can be finished in all sorts of ways to suit a variety of uses. They're not difficult to make, particularly if you get the panels cut to the exact size when you buy the board, doing away with the most time consuming part of the job.

Most timber merchants and larger do-it-yourself stores provide a cutting service, charging only a small fee for each cut made. You need to supply an accurate cutting plan with all the panel measurements – use the one provided overleaf or make your own plan

if you want to alter the dimensions. Otherwise you can cut out the panels by hand, using a panel saw or jigsaw.

The best choice of material for both the box and the cupboard, where all the parts comprise flat panels, is medium density fibreboard (MDF). This is available in large, inexpensive sheets, which are easy to work, have a smooth finish for painting and – once your masterpiece is complete – don't shrink, warp or split. The decorative moulding skirting the sides of the box and trimming the cupboard door is a ready-cut trim, also made of MDF. Cut in a wide range of designs, decorative mouldings are available from some do-it-yourself stores and by mail order.

Put your hand-made box to good use in a hundred and one ways, from storing children's toys or polishing brushes to housing board games or indoor gardening tools.

MAKING A BOX

When deciding on the size of the box or cupboard, consider what it's going to be used for – you need to make sure that it's big enough for its intended purpose. To avoid wastage, try to devise a cutting plan that allows you to cut all the pieces from a single sheet of MDF – this might mean adjusting the overall dimensions of the box slightly.

The box shown here is cut from a standard size 1800 x 600mm (6 x 2ft) sheet of 12mm (½in) thick MDF. If you are adding a decorative moulding, you can adjust the width of the side panels slightly to accommodate a whole number of pattern repeats. All the box panels are joined with secret dowel joints. Buy a pack of 30mm (1¼in) 6mm dowels which includes a dowel twist bit, depth stop and centre points.

MEASURING UP

The box shown here measures 37cm (14½in) square and 28cm (11in) high. To make a box the same size use the cutting plan provided; otherwise make your own scale plan on a sheet of squared paper. You will need to cut one base panel (**A**), four side panels (**B, C, D, E**) and a lid (**F**). The dividers (**G** and **H**) are optional.

To allow for the thickness of the board, panels **D** and **E** are 24mm (⅞in) narrower than panels **B** and **C**. To allow for the thickness of a decorative moulding cut the lid 6mm (¼in) larger than the base all round. To fit inside the box the dividers are cut to the same length as panels **D** and **E** but are 14mm (½in) less high.

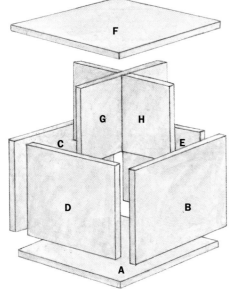

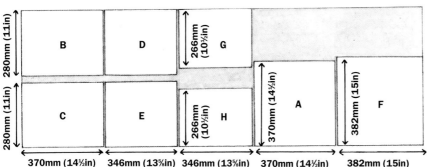

1 **Preparing the panels** Have all the box panels cut out to the plan. Check the sizes and angles; if necessary, trim the edges with a plane. Hold the panels in position and mark the meeting edges so you can match them later. On the side and bottom edges of panels **D** and **E**, mark dowel holes 50mm (2in) from the corners. On the bottom edges of panels **B** and **C**, mark dowel holes 50mm (2in) from the corners and halfway along the edge.

2 **Making the dowel joints** Clamp the panels to a surface and use an electric drill with dowel twist bit and depth stop to drill a 21mm (¾in) deep dowel hole at each mark. Insert a centre point in each hole. Match the meeting edges and press them together to transfer the dowel hole positions. Drill a 9mm (⅜in) deep dowel hole at each centre point mark. Remove the centre points.

3 **Assembling the box** Check all the panels fit together and, if necessary, drill out any dowel holes that are too shallow, drilling into the board edge only. Apply adhesive to the dowels and along the meeting edges and assemble the box. Clamp together with a web clamp or improvised clamp. Remove any excess adhesive with a damp cloth.

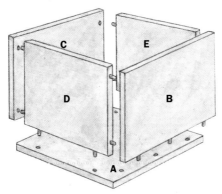

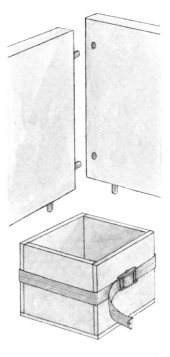

4 **Reinforcing the joints** Avoiding the dowel positions, reinforce the joints with countersunk screws. Fix the screws through the base of the box into the side panels and at the upper edge at the corners – these screws will be hidden or covered with the decorative moulding. Allow the adhesive to dry.

5 **Making the dividers (optional)** Check the dividers fit the box and, if necessary, trim with a plane or abrasive paper. Make a cross-halving joint halfway along both divider pieces, using a panel saw to make the vertical cuts and a chisel to square off the base of the slot. Fit the two pieces together and drop them into the box.

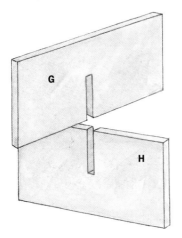

6 **Cutting the moulding (optional)** Use the box as a measuring and cutting guide for the decorative moulding. To match the moulding pattern at the corners, cut moulding for one side, attach it temporarily in place with Blu-tack, then use it as a cutting guide, matching up the pattern repeat, for the adjacent piece. Continue around the box in this way.

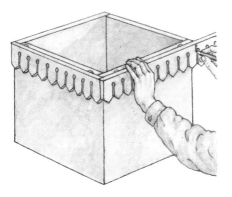

▶ *Piled high with juicy fruits, this brightly painted box might easily steal the limelight from a humble fruit bowl. If you intend to store fruit or vegetables in your box, drill ventilation holes in the lid before painting.*

7 **Making the box lid** Check the lid fits exactly; sand or use a plane to trim the edges if necessary. From MDF offcuts, cut four pieces approximately 5 x 10cm (2 x 4in). Use wood adhesive and 19mm (¾in) panel pins to secure them to the lid underside 19mm (¾in) from the edge as shown.

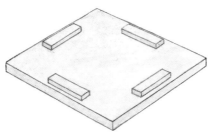

8 **Painting the box and mouldings** Fill any gaps with wood filler and allow to dry. Sand smooth with fine grade abrasive paper then wipe off any dust. Apply primer and leave to dry. Use masking tape to mask different colour areas if necessary and apply two coats of emulsion paint, allowing to dry and sanding lightly between coats.

9 **Finishing off** Secure the moulding around the sides of the box using 12mm (½in) panel pins – two at each corner and two in between. Touch up the nail heads with paint. Apply a coat of clear polyurethane varnish to protect the finish if necessary, and leave the box to dry.

MAKING A CUPBOARD

This cupboard stands 37cm (14¼in) high, is 28cm (11in) wide and 20cm (8in) deep. All the pieces are cut from a standard 1200 x 600mm (4 x 2ft) sheet of MDF following the cutting plan below. The panels are cut and assembled in much the same way as the box on the previous pages, with (**A**) forming the back of the cupboard and (**F**) the cupboard door. The door and back panel are cut to the same size. A shelf (**G**) is fitted with a through housing joint. To allow for the housing joint the shelf is 6mm (¼in) wider than the inside width of the cupboard.

In addition to the tools and materials needed for making a box, you need two flush hinges, a handle and a magnetic door catch.

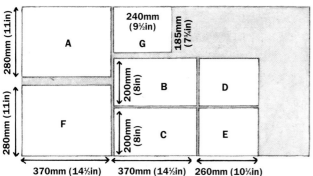

1 Preparing the panels
Have the panels cut to size. Check the size and if necessary trim with a plane. Decide on the shelf height. Hold the shelf in position against the panel **C** and, using a try square to check it's square, mark the shelf width on **C**. Use a tenon saw and chisel to cut a 4mm (⅜in) slot between the marks. Cut an equivalent slot in **B**.

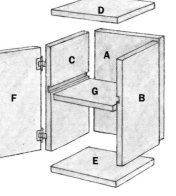

2 Assembling the cupboard Follow steps 1-3 *Making a Box* to assemble the cupboard, taking care to offset the dowel joints between panels **A – B** and **A – C** from the shelf housing joints. Reinforce with countersunk screws through the base and back panel of the cupboard, using two screws on each side. Slide the shelf into place.

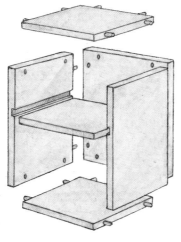

3 Painting the cupboard Check that the door fits flush with the sides of the cupboard and use a plane to trim the edges if necessary. Cut a piece of decorative moulding to fit across the top edge of the door, if desired. Paint the cupboard, handle and any decorative moulding then pin the moulding to the top edge of the door, following steps 8 and 9 *Making a Box*.

◣ *This bright and cheery free-standing cupboard can easily be adapted to make a wall-mounted cabinet. Fix mirror plates to the back panel along the top and bottom edge, then screw the cupboard in place using wallplugs or cavity fixings.*

4 Fixing the door Lay the door face down. Mark hinge positions on one side of door, 5cm (2in) from the top and bottom. Centre the hinges at the marks with the knuckle protruding over the edge and use a bradawl to make pilot holes for the screws. Screw hinges in place. Lay the cupboard on its back and hold the door in place and open. Make pilot holes in the edge of the upright and screw the hinges in place.

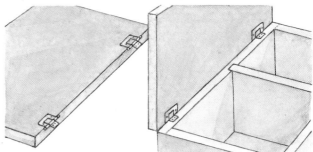

5 Fitting handle and catch Mark the handle position and drill a screw hole at the mark. Fix the handle with the screw supplied. Screw the magnetic catch to the inside edge of the cupboard, and the metal plate to the inside face of the door, so they meet when the door is closed.

DRILLED PATTERNS

*Give an ordinary cupboard an unusual decorative touch
by drilling a pattern of holes on the door. The drilled design is very
straightforward – use the template provided or create your own design.*

A dding a drilled decoration to a cupboard door uses only simple woodworking skills and turns any plain, ordinary cupboard into a special feature. A pierced door looks good on a bathroom or a bedside cabinet, for example, or perhaps a small wall-mounted cupboard in the hall or living room.

The cupboard can be made of natural wood or medium density fibreboard (MDF). You may already have the other items you need, but if not, they are all available from do-it-yourself shops. Use the template provided as a pattern for drilling the holes, enlarging it as necessary to fit your cupboard door.

After drilling the pattern, the cupboard can be painted to suit the decor of any room.

DRILLING A WOODEN DOOR

If you are not going to paint the cupboard, there is no need to remove the existing clear varnish from the surface, but you do need to varnish the insides of the holes to protect them.

While drilling the holes, support the drilled area of the door on a piece of board, to prevent the door from splitting as the drill bit breaks through. The support board should be 12mm (½in) thick and slightly larger than the area being drilled. If your cupboard door has a panel, cut the support board to fit this panel rather than the whole door.

1 Preparing the door Photocopy the template on to a sheet of tracing paper – enlarging if necessary. Unscrew the door from its hinges. Lay the door flat on the work surface. Position the tracing paper pattern on the outside face and secure it with masking tape.

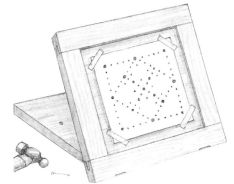

3 Attaching the support board Using the 2mm (½2in) wood bit, drill six holes through the door as indicated by the ringed holes on the pattern. Temporarily attach the door to the support board with No 4 screws through the six

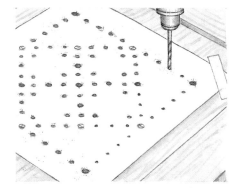

4 Drilling the pattern Using a 4mm (³⁄₁₆in) wood bit, drill through the small holes marked on the pattern. Then switch to a 6mm (¼in) drill bit and drill the larger holes as marked, except those which are being used temporarily to fix the door to the support board.

5 Removing the screws Remove one screw at a time and re-drill each hole with the 6mm (¼in) bit as indicated. Hold the door firmly against the support board, while you drill the very last hole. File round the edges of the holes, then varnish round the inside for a tidy finish.

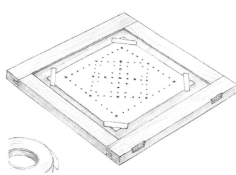

2 Supporting the door Place the door on top of the support board. Using a hammer and nail, make a small indent in the centre of each mark on the pattern to act as a guide for the drill bit and prevent it from slipping. Leave the paper pattern in place while drilling the holes.

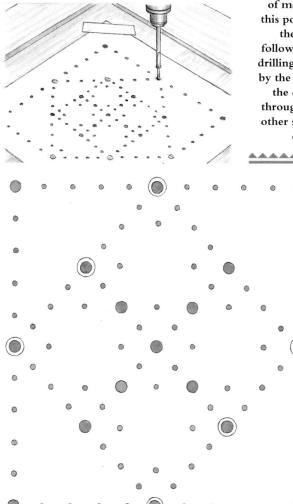

YOU WILL NEED

❖ TRACING PAPER
❖ MASKING TAPE
❖ CHIPBOARD for support
❖ HAMMER AND NAIL
❖ DRILL
❖ WOOD DRILL BITS, 2mm, 4mm and 6mm (½2, ³⁄₁₆, ¼in)
❖ 6 No 4 SCREWS, 20mm (¾in)
❖ SCREWDRIVER
❖ SMALL ROUND FILE
❖ CLEAR VARNISH
❖ SMALL ARTISTS' BRUSH

TIP

DRILLING INTO MDF

If your door is made of MDF, drill from both sides in order to get really clean holes. Drill into the door until the drill bit tip only just reaches through to the other side. Use a small piece of masking tape to mark this point on the drill. Drill the rest of the door, following the template and drilling to the depth marked by the tape each time. Turn the door over and drill through the holes from the other side. File the holes to clean them off.

◀ You can enlarge or copy this template to fit the door on your cupboard. Drill all small holes with a 4mm (³⁄₁₆in)drill bit. Drill all large holes with a 6mm (¼in) bit. The six ringed large holes are drilled first and then used to attach the door to the support board.

STAR QUALITY

Add a sprinkling of stars to your rooms for a quick and easy finishing touch that's stylish, young at heart and right up to date.

S tar motifs are a fun way to add sparkle to your home. There's an abundance of stars around in the shops, from whole constellations printed on wallpaper and furnishing fabrics to dainty star patterns on accessories such as lampshades. You can also buy moulded stars to hang on walls – rather than using them singly, make the most of a few stars by hanging them in clusters of three or five beside a mirror or wall light.

For individual stellar highlights, buy a star stamp from a large stationery store and print a sprinkling of stars around a room. If you like, you could try your hand at making your own star stamp using a potato or lino cut, or glue cut-outs from spare starry gift wrap, wallpaper or fabric on to lampshades. Creating a good star shape is quite simple: draw two triangles, one upside-down over the other, then elongate the points as necessary. Make star templates, and copy them on to card or fabric which you can paint or dye.

Stars and stripes make great partners on this handpainted wall. A cluster of ceramic stars can add sparkle to a ceiling or door as well as walls.

For a starlit glow, look for a lampshade with a starry theme or stencil your own star motif on to a plain shade.

Celestial floor tiles can be set as light relief in an area of plain tiles. If the tiles are as handsome as these, you could display them singly as wall miniatures.

Trinkets with a star motif reinforce the theme.

Star gazing is possible day and night with a galaxy of shimmering stars at the window. White stars, printed on a sheer white voile blind, let in maximum light with starry impact.

Starry highlights are easily introduced with a star stamp – gold or silver stars shine out particularly brightly from a dark background like this rich red wall. To create your own heavenly effects, use a stamp, such as one of those shown on the right, and practise first on spare paper before setting to work on the wall.

FROM THE HEART

*A universal symbol of affection, the simple heart shape,
with its symmetrical, mirror-image curve, can add a romantic
finishing touch to a range of household objects.*

F or thousands of years, the heart was revered as the source of romantic feelings. Though modern science has disproved this and the traditional heart motif is far from anatomically correct, it is instantly accepted as a symbol of warm affection. From frivolous, heart-shaped balloons, chocolate boxes, car bumper stickers and even beds, to the undying love expressed in Valentine's Day cards and lovers' graffiti, the heart symbol transcends all language and cultural barriers. And though the heart motif has feminine overtones, the heart itself has long represented the seat of masculine courage, as well as love.

Heart motifs are often red or pink, but the image is strong enough to remain recognizable in other colours – gold lockets, for example – and as a small, integral part of a larger object or pattern. The motif features in Pennsylvania Dutch, Swiss and German arts and crafts but is also found in Gothic tracery patterns and ancient Greek friezes. It is ideal for stencilling, hand painting and quilting. For instant topiary, grow ivy up a heart-shaped support; for a touch of pure Victoriana, grow hardy herbaceous perennial bleeding hearts (*Dicentra* species and varieties), with their locket-shaped blooms, in the garden.

*The heart motif is
the central focal
point of this fanciful
wirework wall
basket, emphasizing
the symmetry of the
object and pointing
to its decorative
contents below.*

◀ **This little bird box** in robin-redbreast colours features an iron heart-shaped plaque around the front entrance hole.

◢ **Rows of alternating** large and small gold hearts add a quirky touch of warmth to the front of a simple open cupboard.

◢ **Wirework kitchenware,** such as these heart baskets, with their delicate, ornamental curls, make unusual storage containers.

◥ **Formal stripes** and fanciful hearts combine on this appliquéd patchwork coverlet to produce an eye-catching throw.

WRITTEN DETAILS

Well-versed homes are decorated with writing – on the walls, lampshades, bedlinen and even china. This new fashion for decorating articles for the home with beautiful script draws on time-honoured traditions.

The ability to write an elegant script was – and still is – a highly regarded skill. The exquisite manuscripts of the Middle Ages ensured that calligraphy (the art of beautiful writing) gained a well-deserved place alongside other fine arts.

The skill of fine calligraphy was almost lost with the development of printed type, while in this century the value placed on the ability to write gracefully has also diminished. Changing social conventions, cou-pled with the widespread use of typewriters and word processors, mean that handwriting is rarely seen.

Current decorating trends are set to change this as once again calligraphy is in favour. There are many applications for calligraphy in the home. Flowing scripts are used to decorate fabrics, monograms personalize items and old letters, especially those with a family history, are framed for their character as much as sentimental value.

An inexpensive storage box receives a special makeover, with hand-written descriptions of the contents painted on the front of each small drawer.

◀ **Preserve the sense of romance** that surrounds old hand-written letters and postcards by framing them. Stark modern photograph frames, such as these, contrast brilliantly with the faded quality of the ink and yellow, aged appearance of the writing paper.

☑ **What could be more appropriate** than to cover a desk set with wrapping paper printed with fine calligraphy? Once varnished, new paper used this way looks antique.

☑ **China takes on a timeless look** appropriately decorated with food-linked words. Even though these letters are printed, their graceful lines provide a handworked look.

▲ **Tight lines** of well-formed writing are drawn directly on plain white bedlinen. Modern fabric pens, in a wide range of colours, make writing on fabric just as easy as putting pen to paper.

MUSICAL SCORES

You don't need to be musical, or even know how to read music, to enjoy the flowing graphic images of musical notation.

Music is an international language which cuts across all sorts of boundaries – social, economic, cultural, generational – uniting people in their listening enjoyment. Musical scores, with their instantly recognizable, orderly notation, are equally universal, and they can be used in a variety of ways in the home – you don't even need to be able to read music to appreciate them.

The basic musical notation consists of a staff – the system of equally spaced, parallel horizontal lines grouped into sets of five – upon which the musical notes are written. At the left-hand side of each staff, a bass or treble clef, or other symbol, indicates the pitch of music, while the notes themselves indicate the pitch and duration of each musical sound.

As motifs, they can have an effect ranging from formal and serious, in the case of elaborately framed, valuable antique scores, to light-hearted, such as hand-painted, grafitti-like notes wafting across a child's bedroom wall, with cartoon characters playing musical instruments.

If you are musically orientated and have a room or corner devoted to music, hang portraits of favourite composers or musicians, framed sheets of music or prints of instruments. Groups of notes are ideal for a frieze, stencilled at cornice height or, on a smaller scale, worked in needlepoint for a cushion cover. Old sheet music can still be bought quite reasonably from antique markets and specialist shops – or try making your own antique look with a slight wash of weak tea.

This music lover's corner features a violin, a painting of a violin and carefully pleated sheet music glued to flower pots, creating a cachepot effect for a dried flower display.

▶ Upbeat and unusual, this pair of wrought iron candle sconces, based on musical notation motifs, look best against a plain background.

▲ Old, yellowed ballet scores are used as translucent shades for door windows and a lamp, and opaquely to cover a bulletin board frame and lamp base. Ballet books and photographs reinforce the theme.

▼ Larger than life musical notes on a mottled pink background give this glazed ceramic tea setting a jazzy look.

◤ Do-it-yourself, with an indelible ink fabric pen: this cushion cover features a favourite piece of music, hand written on plain fabric.

SHADOW PLAY

Cleverly cut silhouette portraits make a charming display and are an attractive and original alternative to family snapshots. Good likenesses are easy to achieve once you know how.

In the days preceding photography, shadow portraits were a decorative and inexpensive way to record family likenesses. Though some skilled craftsmen could cut the silhouettes freehand, most shadow portraits were produced by tracing the life-size shadow of the subject on to a sheet of paper, then reducing it using a special drawing tool and filling it in with black ink.

You can create your own shadow portraits using a similar technique. Use an unshaded table lamp to cast your subject's shadow on to a sheet of paper pinned to the wall; trace around the shadow,

then reduce the outline on a photocopier and cut it from black paper. Alternatively, you can trace around figures on a photograph – this is a good way to create full-figure silhouettes.

You can mount your silhouette portraits in lots of different ways. White and ivory are traditional background colours, or you could use sepia to create a time-worn appearance or a bold, primary colour for modern surroundings. If you want to use silhouette portraits as a design motif in your home, try stencilling them on to the walls or use a fabric with silhouette motifs, as shown overleaf.

Immortalize friends, relatives and even favourite pets by cutting their shadow portrait from black paper. Framed and set against a richly coloured wallpaper, these two silhouettes make a handsome display.

▶ *Two dancing figures* form a pretty silhouette on a white candlelamp shade. They were stencilled in place, but you could create a similar look on a plain shade by sticking a silhouette cut out from black paper on it.

◀ *Flickering candlelight* casts a warm glow across the intricate silhouette of this belle of the ball. She stands out well against the background of a gold-painted candle sconce.

▼ *Children at play* and distinguished gentlemen are the subjects of this handsome collection of framed Victorian shadow portraits. Note how some of the gentlemen's collars have been left un-inked — shadow portraitists of the time often highlighted details in this way.

▶ *Stencilled silhouette* portraits are a clever variation on a theme. Here, even the frames and mounts have been stencilled directly on to the wall. The lady's elegant silhouette has been painted in white to give an attractive cameo effect.

HERALDIC MOTIFS

The distinctive shapes and rich colours of heraldic motifs can be used purely ornamentally – to give historic overtones and even a hint of ancient pedigree – to a traditional decor.

Heraldry – the display and study of coats of arms – dates back to the early development of armour, when solid plate replaced chain mail and helmets became larger, for increased protection. To be able to identify friends and foes in battle, an insignia was marked on each soldier's shield and on a flag-like banner. The insignia was also useful for documentation in times when few people could read their names. By Elizabethan times, coats of arms were regarded as the mark of a gentleman, passing from one generation to the next.

Heraldry today is a huge, complex subject, with its own descriptive language; whole books are devoted to explaining how to describe, or blazon, a coat of arms. You needn't be an expert, however, to make decorative use of heraldic motifs, in stencilling, hand-painting, printed fabric or even stained glass.

Popular heraldic devices include real and mythical creatures such as boars, stags, eagles, unicorns, griffins, dragons, lions, horses and swans; natural phenomena such as stars, moons and suns; objects such as spears, harps and keys and geometric shapes such as crosses, stripes and chevrons. Royal motifs include the crown and the fleur de lys – resembling an iris, the head of a sceptre or battle axe, this is also called the flower of Luce or heraldic lily and has long symbolized French royalty.

Whatever motif you choose, keep shapes simple, and colours rich – gold, silver, red, blue, black, green and purple are traditional heraldic colours.

Heraldry has rich, historical overtones. This row of hand-painted, wall-hung wooden shields reinforces the medieval richness of the decor. The fleur de lys candle sconce (left) is a characteristic heraldic motif.

85

▲ *The most heraldic of beasts*, this canvaswork lion is standing, or statant in blazonry terms. Lions can also be rampant, on raised back legs; sejant, sitting; couchant, lying down with head erect, looking forwards; or dormant, lying down with head on forepaws.

◳ *Fleur de lys motifs*, stencilled in gold, enliven plain painted or paint-effect walls; crenellated pelmets and fleur de lys finials add to the theme.

▲ *Lifesize,* stencilled medieval knights, set in Gothic tracery niches, are surmounted by heraldic shields.

◼ *Knights in shining armour* charge over wallpaper and furnishing fabric – perfect for a young boy's room.

BUTTERFLIES

As light as air and as luminous as jewels, butterflies capture the exquisite perfection of nature, and butterfly motifs can bring that ethereal perfection indoors.

In Victorian times collecting butterflies, like collecting birds' eggs, was seen as a worthy scientific pursuit for professional and amateur alike, and countless specimens ended up in display cases. Today's fascination with wildlife is as strong as ever, but attitudes have changed and capturing butterflies on film has replaced capturing them physically.

Many habitats for butterflies are now protected and plants that attract butterflies are sold in garden centres and seed catalogues. There are even butterfly farms which breed native and tropical species, for sale as eggs or caterpillars, and which display live butterflies in their recreated natural environments.

In terms of decor, there are two- and three-dimensional options for bringing butterflies to life. Hand-coloured Victorian prints and book illustrations look lovely framed on their own or displayed as a collection. Photographs, especially if you have taken them yourself, and natural history posters have a more modern look. Wallpaper, fabrics and china can be decorated solely with butterfly motifs, or a mixture of butterflies and flowers. China butterflies, life-size or larger, can rest delicately on a house plant for a pretty finishing touch; and in a children's room, larger-than-life butterfly mobiles and kites can hover gently in the air.

◤ *Options for butterfly motifs are numerous, as this delightful group of hand-coloured prints and needlework samplers shows.*

◤ *A hand-painted, glazed ceramic butterfly can hover above a house plant or alight permanently on a wall.*

87

◢ A portrait of a butterfly, hung with a gilt-flecked rope, makes an unusual and startlingly beautiful showpiece.

◣ A group of butterflies, in the form of hand-painted plates, can hover around a bedroom mirror or, as seen in this mirror's reflection, around a picture.

◢ Flowers and butterflies are inseparable, since flowers provide the nectar on which butterflies feed. Here a hand-painted jug with simple butterfly motifs is filled with summery pink weigela and white hydrangea blossom.

◣ Combining old and new, these Victorian butterfly prints appear to float in their modern glass and beechwood frames.

SHELL DELIGHT

*Collected on long walks along the shore,
shells come in a wonderful range of shapes and colours – use
them to bring a breath of fresh sea air into your home.*

Shells come in all sorts of wonderful shapes, and their marvellous natural colours blend in with almost any colour scheme in the home. The bathroom is the obvious place to use them, but they can add a fine finishing touch to almost any room. As well as real shells, you can extend the theme with furnishings, wallcoverings, decorations, ornaments and accessories based on shell designs.

Small shells look best in groups; large ones can be grouped or displayed on their own. You can use them to decorate just about anything, from mirrors and lampshades to walls, wardrobes and curtains, while large, flat shells

such as scallops make attractive holders for soap, bath pearls, pot-pourri and candles.

Shells are so beautiful they make lovely ornaments in their own right. Display them where there is plenty of light. Windowsills are ideal places, or you can backlight them on shelves. Displaying shells in water – in a goldfish bowl or tropical fish tank, or even just a pretty glass jug – makes their colours more vivid.

But much of the pleasure of shells is in handling them: leave one or two around where you can pick them up, and hold them to your ear to hear the sea and take yourself back to long summer holidays spent on the beach.

This treasure trove from far flung shores includes exotic shells and prints. Shells washed up on the beach are bleached to pastel shades by the sun and sea air. Here, pale green driftwood frames and a weatherbeaten light blue cupboard complete the scene.

◄ *On a seaside theme*, this needlepoint cushion depicts some beautifully worked shells.

◄ *The delicate translucency* of small shells shows up best in natural light. This is brilliantly exploited here by sewing them to a white sheer curtain.

▲ *Beachcombing finds*, framed and displayed in groups, bring back memories of seaside holidays.

◄ *Like a lobster pot*, a plain wicker basket makes a good container for shells.

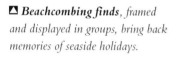

▲ *On the fun side*, elaborate on the shell theme with bathroom novelties such as these colourful soaps.

◄ *A few seashells* add a decorative touch to a plain terracotta pot – simply glue one or two of your favourite shells in place along the rim.

◄ *Oyster shell candles* are marvellous for lighting romantic dinners for two, and are also the perfect accompaniment to a relaxing bath.

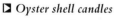

WATERING CANS

*Display decorative, old-fashioned, painted
metal watering cans indoors and out, to add a splash
of colour to a setting.*

With the growing popularity of conservatories and patios, the boundaries between house and garden have become increasingly hazy. House plants and fresh and dried flower arrangements have long been used to bring a touch of the garden indoors but you can also use traditional gardening accessories such as wooden trugs, wicker baskets and watering cans to add a garden-like atmosphere.

When it comes to the choice of material, metal is a must. Plastic may be efficient but lacks any nostalgic quality. Modern galvanized metal garden watering cans and smaller, copper or enamelled metal watering cans for house plants are available at garden centres and do-it-yourself stores, but if you can get a secondhand, rust-free watering can, so much the better. Scour junk shops, flea markets and jumble/garage sales. Using oil-based enamels or car spray paint, you can stencil or hand-paint fruit, flower or leaf motifs on to the can.

To add to the outdoor theme you can use the watering can as a cachepot, filling the top hole with a trailing or arching house plant such as Boston fern; if need be, pack the can first with crumpled newspaper or peat to correct the levels.

Lastly, if you're keen on collecting Victoriana, as well as garden watering cans, look out for charming little indoor watering cans, also known as watering pots, made out of various metals. These were filled with perfumed water, which was sprinkled over artificial wax or porcelain flowers in indoor arrangements.

Watering cans have a natural affinity with flowers and foliage. Indoors, consider displaying them surrounded by house plants.

△ Galvanized metal watering can and cake moulds *serve as containers for a garden of shasta daisies. Their cut stems are imbedded in saturated florists' foam, the surface of which is covered with moss.*

△ Blazing colours *from watering cans can enhance the garden scene as successfully as flowers. By respraying the can you can change its colour as often as you like.*

▶ A modest collection *of weather-worn, metal watering cans, in a variety of shapes, makes a pretty feature in combination with an equally weather-worn wooden chest.*

▽ Hand–painted fruit *adds a touch of class to this galvanized watering can. You can use scrupulously clean watering cans as instant, if unconventional, ice buckets.*

GARDEN TRUGS

Humble in origin and once confined to the shed, wooden trugs are now fashionable interior accessories, ideal for bringing a sense of the garden indoors.

I nvented in the 1820s, garden trugs were handmade of planed wood or wicker without any ornamental aspirations. They were designed in different shapes and sizes – rectangular or round, shallow or deep – and with a variety of handle shapes. The smallest trugs were used for gathering grapes from the greenhouse and larger ones for collecting vegetables.

Today, garden trugs have a special appeal – they encapsulate the nostalgic qualities of cottage gardens. As containers for informal flower displays, trugs can make even the most obvious florists' flowers look fresh from the garden. Use a florists' foam block as the foundation, lining the trug first with plastic or resting the foam block in a cheap, fitting plastic tray. For an informal effect, insert the lower stems horizontally or angled slightly downwards so they overhang the rim, then gradually build density upwards.

Trugs are equally useful as room tidies for small household objects liable to be misplaced, whether in the kitchen, bathroom, workshop or even on a desk. A ceiling-hung collection would enhance any country decor. Buy new wooden and wicker trugs from most garden centres and look for old ones at garage sales, junk shops and flea markets, where they can sometimes be had, complete with the extra character imbued by long use, for a proverbial song.

Wooden trugs are ideal for informal flower arrangements. This unusual summer display features delicate herb blossom, including fennel, mint, marjoram, dill, feverfew and brilliant blue borage.

◄ **Pretty polyanthus,** still in their pots, fill this traditional trug; other inexpensive seasonal bedding-plant alternatives include English daisies, pansies, busy Lizzies or, for drama, one big ornamental cabbage.

◢ **A lovely windowsill vignette** is created with a trug and homemade preserves, herbal oil, pots of fresh herbs and wooden scoops. The fresh sunflower shown is short-lived, but a paper or silk sunflower could be substituted.

◢ **A shallow trug on legs** provides easy access to fresh vegetables. For an instant seasonal display, fill a trug with fresh vegetables, fruits or ornamental gourds, then add a few nuts or sprigs of bay leaves.

◢ **Weather-worn,** this old garden trug with its pale brown patina makes a perfect, floor-level hold-all in a bathroom based on soft, earthy tones.

WIREWORKS

Linear, airy and elegant, wirework utensils and ornaments always add a light-hearted, decorative finishing touch to a decor – and many are surprisingly practical.

V aguely French in feeling, small wirework items manage to combine elegance with a touch of humour. Even though they are manufactured – traditionally of mild steel dipped in anti-corrosive chrome, nickel or tin – a slight unevenness gives them a timeless, handmade appeal; and the small dents and irregularities that develop with age and use only add to their charm.

Display them against white or solid colours, where their tracery can be seen to advantage, especially if they can catch and reflect the light.

Most are modestly priced, so you can build up a collection to hang on a wall or fill a shelf or tabletop. Because wirework is so delicate, the items are also ideal foils to contrast with chunky earthenware pottery, natural wooden bowls or enamelled cast ironware.

Wirework can quickly get dusty and, especially in a kitchen, greasy. To keep it looking its best, brush off loose dirt, wash quickly in hot detergent, using a soft brush if necessary, then rinse and leave to dry thoroughly in a warm place.

Three polyanthus-filled terracotta flowerpots set off the delicate tracery of this charming wirework planter, complete with dainty feet and heart motif.

As lively and unsophisticated as a child's drawing, these wirework, chicken- and duck-shaped egg holders make pleasant kitchen companions, and could equally well hold fruit or vegetables.

▲ **Make your own wirework,** based on simple motifs, out of coat-hanger or other flexible narrow-gauge wire. This homemade towel rail 'with a heart' would make a lovely house-warming present.

▶ **For a spring garden effect** in miniature, pack the space between flowerpots in a wirework planter with fresh sphagnum moss, or place a vase of cut flowers in a moss-packed wirework outer container.

◀ **Raised wirework** candle-glass holders create a dark, lacy, web-like effect seen against the softly translucent wax.

▼ **Wirework accessories** for the bathroom combine charm and practicality: this pretty fish-motif soapdish allows for easy drainage and the basket makes a well ventilated hold-all for guests' hand towels.

BIRD CAGES

Bird cages derive their appeal from diminutive perfection and, even empty, their delicate tracery and architectural form capture the imagination.

Pet birds, with their exotic beauty, melodious song and mimicry, have fascinated people for centuries; their cages often reflected contemporary taste and architecture, as well as hinting at their owner's wealth. If you dislike the idea of keeping live birds in captivity, however, or just don't want the bother of looking after a pet, you can still display their cages to decorative advantage. They range from delicate, close-barred houses for finches to huge cages for parrots, and from simple box shapes to multi-tiered, ornate palaces. Made of metal wire – brass was a Victorian favourite – bamboo or wood, bird cages are sold in pet shops, antique and Oriental shops.

You can display bird cages in halls, conservatories, living rooms – anywhere a bare wall calls for a bit of linear detail, or the decor requires a touch of whimsy. Rest the cages on tables, hang them from purpose-built or improvised stands, from brackets on a wall or from the rafters, individually or in carefully composed groups.

For a jovial effect, you can put model birds inside – choose from life-like porcelain reproductions, ethnic, hand-carved and painted wooden birds or inexpensive Oriental ornamental birds with real feathers. Alternatively, you can use the cage to house a small-leaved trailing house plant – an asparagus fern, ivy or plant with long, trailing runners such as mother-of-thousands or spider plant. Try to relate the size and scale of the plant to the size of the cage and spacing of the bars.

A magical effect is created by wall-hung, table top and free-standing tiny bird cages containing night lights illuminating the entrance to a home. The treatment would be equally enchanting lighting up a summer evening party on a patio.

► *The delicacy* of handmade bird cages is best appreciated in uncluttered settings – pale for dark wood or metal cages, dark for pale ones.

▼ *With dolls' house overtones,* this bird cage rests on a landing halfway up a flight of stairs. Cages with strong architectural overtones such as this require no occupant to make their point.

▲ *Have fun with fakes*, such as this pair of bluebird cut-outs flitting to the outside of their free-standing cage, and fantasy caged bird brooding nearby.

▼ *Looking like a rajah's palace,* this bird cage is filled with wandering Jew (Zebrina pendula). Ensure you can reach plants in bird cages for watering and care.

MINIATURE HOUSES

Whether you possess a beloved dolls' house that you played with as a child, or are simply fascinated by a miniature world of tiny rooms and pint-sized furniture, a dolls' house is a great conversation piece to display in your home.

The first recorded dolls' house was made in Bavaria in 1558 for the Duke of Albrecht's daughter. The early dolls' houses were known as baby houses. They were masterpieces of craftsmanship, hung with rich tapestries and stocked with the finest furniture and exquisite china, all made to perfect scale in miniature. Such works of art were more likely to be displayed in the living room or dining room than in the playroom or nursery. To this day, the living room is still one of the best places to keep a much-loved dolls' house on show to family and friends.

Owning a dolls' house can become an absorbing hobby, whether you regard your 'second home' as a mini replica of a real house for experimenting with design ideas, or as an adult plaything for displaying a beautiful collection of model furniture. There are several options open – you can buy new, build your own from scratch or using a kit, or hunt down a good second-hand one at an auction or car boot sale. Your ingenuity and specialist dolls' house suppliers provide everything you need for making or restoring a dolls' house, from sheets of tiny brick or slate tile patterned paper and scaled down wallpaper patterns to miniaturized furniture, accessories and even pets.

A desirable residence by any standards, a handsome dolls' house with a Georgian façade nestles neatly into the fireside alcove, where anyone sitting in the living room can admire it.

▶ In estate agents' terms, location is all important to a property. Here, a three-storey dolls' house becomes an admirable focal point of the room, by doubling as a firescreen in front of an empty grate.

▼ The wide open spaces of a conservatory, looking through to the lawn beyond, give this dolls' cottage a realistic country setting. For the front garden, a gravel path winds up through a jungle of pot plants to the front door that is left invitingly ajar. Pot plants are just the right scale to look like trees screening the cottage from the road.

▲ Just as in real life, the lady of the dolls' house waits at her front door to greet her guests – or to wave them goodbye. The teddy bear on the chair suggests a child's room, but it could equally well be a hallway.

HATS ON DISPLAY

What do you do with a summery straw hat when you're not wearing it? Don't hide it away in a box – use it to bring a touch of summer freshness into your home. It might become a permanent feature of your decor.

With their attractive tones and textures, straw hats are made for adorning with dried or fabric flowers to create pretty objects that are perfect for enhancing country-style rooms. Trimmed with vibrant blooms and ribbons, they add a splash of colour to plain walls or corners. Mix flowers with ribbons and artificial or dried leaves to complement the overall colour scheme of your room and add a delicate feminine touch.

Straw hats with interesting weaves and generous brims look especially effective exhibited on walls in any country-style room. Hanging wide-brimmed hats decorated with fresh summer flowers and finished off with a floppy ribbon bow captures the country garden scene. Straw boaters, decked with small dried flowers, have a stronger, more angular shape and look good displayed flat on cabinets. They also make an eye-catching arrangement propped up on dresser shelves.

Other ideas include giving a nostalgic feel to a bedroom with miniature straw hats on old-fashioned china dolls, or brightening up a hallway wall with a row of small hats linked by a wide, lush ribbon. If you decide to use purely decorative hats, hang ones you actually wear between them for a really fun effect.

Add elegance and style to a traditional-style dressing table by displaying lovely veiled and flower-bedecked hats on decorative wooden hatstands.

🔺 *A small straw boater* with a rim of pink and red fabric anemones helps add a light, feminine touch to this desk. Note how the fabric flowers tone in with the rose decorations and floral stationery.

🔺 *A delicately woven straw hat,* decorated with dusky dried roses and complementary pink ribbon bows, is very much in keeping with this summer house setting, evoking images of heady, sunny days.

◀ *Peach and pink fabric flowers* are cleverly combined with shiny artificial fruit and dried leaves on this rustic-looking hat. The final effect harmonizes with the fruit pattern of the curtains and wallcoverings.

🔻 *Small is beautiful* – miniature hats look charming nestling beside a traditionally dressed child's doll.

CLOCK STYLE

*A clock ticking away quietly on a mantelpiece or side table
is one of the traditional reassurances of life, combining beauty,
practicality and often a touch of nostalgia.*

Although digital clocks, with their perfect time-keeping, are part of modern life, and often just one small function of a larger appliance – a music centre, for example, or a computer or microwave – there's something very comforting about a traditional free-standing clock. Its weight, solidity and style hark back to a time when life was more leisurely – even the hands and Roman or Arabic numerals are reassuring – and a ticking or chiming clock can provide a gently soothing background sound.

Though clocks first appeared in the 17th century, when the spring balance and pendulum were invented, they were first manufactured in great numbers during the 19th century. Small mantel and carriage clocks replaced larger long-case styles; carriage clocks with handles were especially popular, as most families could only afford one clock, which was carried from room to room, as well as being taken in carriages when the family travelled.

The Victorians, ever inventive, produced clocks in a range of styles. Cases were made of brass, china and porcelain, ormolu, marble and wood, including rosewood, walnut, ebony and mahogany. Some clocks had protective glass domes; others had matching vases inspired by Dresden china; others still chimed or played music. Some were so elaborate that the face was all but camouflaged.

You can buy originals, reproductions or more modern clocks, but whatever style you choose, try to buy a clock in working order, as repairs can be costly.

Reinforcing the classical theme of the surrounding decor – prints, bust, plaster casts and cherub hatstand – this antique clock is housed in a classical temple in miniature, complete with inlaid brass columns.

◀ *The sinuous curves* and ornate detail of this blue and white china clock echo the curves of the fireplace surround; the mantel mirror reflects the clock's attractive backplate.

◀ *This bracket clock,* with its pale wood and floral-painted face, is ideal for a cottage-style decor. Bracket clocks were placed on tables and mantelpieces as well as brackets, and operated on spring-driven mechanisms.

▲ *With its warm, rich hues* of browns and gold, this classic carriage clock is an attractive focal point in the room and provides a striking contrast to the blue and white chinaware also adorning the mantelpiece.

▶ *In modern style,* this rough-hewn, stone-effect mantel clock combines stark geometry with a traditional gilt face and elegant hands. The frame indentations echo those of the marble fireplace.

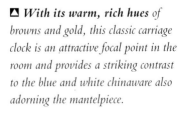

TEAPOT DISPLAYS

*Symbols of domestic comfort and hospitality ranging from
formal to cosy, teapots, tea sets and teatime motifs can form the
basis of a charmingly mixed display.*

For generations, the traditional cup of tea has been the soothing solution to many a crisis. And though loose tea and teapots have often been replaced by teabags brewed in the cup, there's something comforting and timelessly reassuring about an old, much used teapot. One that's been in the family for years often has special sentimental value but you can create a similar effect with antique or second-hand teapots or modern reproductions.

Two or three teapots can comprise a mini-collection, or you can expand as far as funds and horizontal surfaces allow. Display any teapots that catch your fancy or stick to a single style such as Victorian, or a single material such as earthenware, porcelain, pewter, electroplated silver or silver. Alternatively, you can concentrate on one manufacturer such as Wedgwood; one ceramic designer such as Susie Cooper; one colour or colour combination such as royal blue and white; or even one theme – floral-decorated teapots, for example, or animal-shaped ones. Modern, unadorned earthenware and china teapots can be elegant in their simplicity, especially if they are patterned on traditional shapes. Ornamented teapots can be exquisite, but try to avoid excessive fussiness.

Teapot collections are obviously at home in a dining room or kitchen, but they can also enhance a living room or even a bedroom – early morning tea in bed is as traditional as afternoon tea. Matching cups, saucers, creamers and sugar bowls can form part of a display. If space is limited, enlarge your collection two-dimensionally, with wall-hung prints, paintings or samplers of teapots, or even tea trays, and tablecloths printed with teatime motifs.

Steeped in tradition, afternoon tea is a daily, restful and eminently civilized ritual. This collection of two- and three-dimensional teatime memorabilia – teapots, tea caddies, cups and saucers, wall-hung trays with teatime motifs, teacup-printed tea towels and teatime sampler – forms a delightfully domestic corner shrine.

◀ *China teapots,* arranged in a welcoming display, transform a kitchen dresser into an attractive focal point. Highly decorative, the teapots comprise a wide variety of shapes, styles and colours, but all share a country cottage theme.

◢ *Modern teapots,* in keeping with today's fashion for fruit teas, often feature hand-painted summer fruits.

◢ *Formal tea trays* are highly desirable teatime accessories. This dark wood tray with silver handles strikes a handsome contrast to the white porcelain and cloth.

◀ *Directors' chairs* in fabric printed with teapots, cups and saucers, a similar, mini-print tablecloth, and overcloth and napkins appliquéd with teapot motifs ensure that afternoon tea is a light-hearted occasion.

BLUE AND WHITE

With its timeless appeal and ability to blend into almost any setting, blue and white china is as valuable for decoration as it is for practical use and, with a little planning, it can do both beautifully.

Restful and appealing to the eyes, blue and white china has a fresh, clean-looking charm. Hiding it away behind cupboard doors is a waste of obvious display potential. It looks most attractive exhibited on walls and can be shown off to great effect on shelves or tables.

When displaying the china, try to choose a well lit space, safe from accidental knocks. Pieces with hairline cracks, unsuitable for the rough and tumble of daily use, are ideal for a permanent, high-level display.

Blue and white china spans every price bracket and many styles, cultures and periods, including modern, reproduction or genuine antique. There are traditional English designs such as Willow pattern or Oriental Pheasant, as well as Mediterranean, Dutch, Persian or Oriental designs. You can concentrate on a single design, with interest coming from the varied shapes and sizes, or display a mixture. Arrange them symmetrically or as a random patchwork of china sharing only the common colour theme.

Fresh garden flowers add subtle colour to this set of china with its delicate, pale-blue Oriental theme, displayed formally on matching blue painted shelves.

 **Spongeware jugs** and Victorian floral transfer-printed china join forces with a royal-blue jug, white flowers and blue and white fabrics for a cheerful domestic ensemble.

 **Glass fronted** white wooden cupboards with display lighting provide a bright setting for a collection of well-loved china. The blue and white theme is picked up again in stencils.

 **A mix-and-match collection** of old blue and white serving plates and lids enlivens a high stair wall, with room up the stairs for further items as the collection expands.

 **Inexpensive Chinese cachepots** conceal plastic flowerpots perfectly, prevent water staining the table and add unity and elegance to grouped house-plant displays. In summer, you can move them outside to liven up a patio.

GLASS ACT

Arranged with flair in a cleverly lit spot, a collection of tinted glass – whether in brilliant primary hues or frosted pastel tones – brings a touch of colour into a room.

With coloured glass you're never limited to just one display option – there is always room for variation. You can create a perfectly rounded display with only two or three pieces or continue adding to and upgrading your collection, until it becomes the main focal point of a room.

Though some coloured glass is extremely costly because of its antique or rarity value, the raw material itself, made of sand and soda or potash, is plentiful. Well-designed, coloured glass can be surprisingly cheap – look in museum shops, which sell good reproductions. Also look out for attractive glassware in junk shops and at garage sales – you might find a treasure at a bargain price.

Experiment with combinations of different glassware. Try a group of differently shaped pieces in one colour for a dramatic look, or display glass items of complementary tones with colourless pieces for a softer mood. A simple arrangement of a pair of candlesticks or two identical flask-shaped vases creates a formal symmetrical effect which is ideal for a mantelpiece.

Glass is especially enhanced by good lighting; transparent glass looks fantastic set against a windowsill or on a well-lit shelf.

Fresh blue and green transparent glassware makes up the bulk of this display, set in a toning, colour-rubbed wood and glass cabinet. Clear glass vases, some containing decorative objects, add an extra dimension.

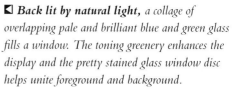

◄ Back lit by natural light, a collage of overlapping pale and brilliant blue and green glass fills a window. The toning greenery enhances the display and the pretty stained glass window disc helps unite foreground and background.

▼ Stark, angular silhouettes and an unusual combination of blue, lilac, mauve and fresh green frosted glass produce a distinctly modern look in this tightly clustered mantelpiece display. The natural form and intricate outline of massed fresh lavender offers welcome contrast in scale and texture.

▲ Classic and contemporary, transparent and frosted glass vases, goblets and candleholders in delicate pale pinks are displayed in rows, while the green leaves of the tulips add a pleasing touch of contrast.

▶ Shimmering glass pebbles provide attractive support for the stems of cut flowers in a clear glass vase. Here, the translucent shades of the pebbles enhance the delicate hues of the flowers.

ALL THAT GLISTERS

All that glisters may well be gold, as gilding – the craft of applying wafer thin sheets of gold to home accessories and furniture – takes off and affordable items are more readily available.

A hint of gold brings a touch of formal elegance and a rich, warm glow to a room. Once seen only in stately homes and palaces, gilded pieces of furniture and accessories, such as elaborately carved picture frames, reflected the wealth and status of the household. Yet the warmth and decorative appeal of these items, gently burnished with gold, is as fitting in many modern homes.

Use gilded items as an accent in a warm, cluttered traditional scheme or opt for a more Scandinavian approach – touches of gold look spectacular in a pale, airy room. Gold is also the the obvious choice for a glamorous film star setting, where it adds to the room's sparkle and sense of luxury.

Antique gilded items are costly and the authentic reproductions are often as highly priced, yet it is pleasantly surprising just how affordable smaller accessories are. Start with a simple mirror or picture frame and build up a collection of nick-nacks and other ornaments brushed with gold. Group them together, including some other items that are not gilded to provide a flattering contrast.

Source your gilded treasures from furniture, department and decorating stores. Or try your hand at gilding to add a golden glow to accessories you already have – gold leaf is sold by some craft and hobby stores. It's possible to cheat too, using gold wax and paint to achieve instant gold effects.

Gold leaf is often applied over a layer of red bolle to enhance its rich tones. Reinforce this link by displaying a collection of golden ornaments alongside red accessories – tiny lacquered trinket boxes and the faded russet of berberis foliage both work to bring the other gold items to life.

▲ *A miniature perfection*, this handsome mirror, modelled in an eighteenth-century style, is only 23cm (9in) high but has all the good looks of a larger, more costly one.

◀ *Glimmers of gold* give a lift to light and airy rooms washed in pale colours. Here a small table brushed with a golden finish and bold-gold picture frames both bring depth to the soft green setting.

▲ *Smaller gilded frames* are a versatile home accessory – they display family photographs to advantage and the accent of gold adds welcome warmth to a tabletop or mantelpiece display.

▼ *For a gold leaf tea*, set a sumptuous tea table with this gilded tea tray, decorated with two cherubic angels – a detail from Madonna Sistina by Raphael.

▲ *Add a decorative edge* to a simple shelf with a carved moulding, painted a rich gold. The glistening gold catches the light to enhance the carving on the moulding.

STERLING CHOICES

*An artful arrangement of silver, whether a simple group of picture frames,
an elaborate table setting or a collection of antique treasures,
adds a touch of classic elegance to any interior.*

G leaming silver, with its timeless appeal, has a place in every home, adding an element of grace and style to both modern and traditional surroundings. Ideal for dressing up a mantelpiece, or table tops and alcove shelving in the living room, silver objects also make excellent bright accessories for the bedroom and bathroom.

Even a single piece of silver, when carefully positioned, lends elegance and interest to a room. In a guest room, for example, a delicate posy of flowers arranged in a little silver vase creates a welcoming touch, while a shiny silver christening mug, catching the light on a windowsill or reflected in a mantelpiece mirror, enhances the formal look of a living room.

A selection of small silver items, whether genuine antique curios or reproduction pieces, placed on an occasional table for instance, forms an interesting focal point. Victorian-style trinkets, such as card cases, pill boxes and match box covers make perfect display material, as do collections of thimbles and teaspoons.

A group of freestanding silver picture frames also makes an attractive tableau. Whether you choose plain or ornate styles, the frames provide continuity for a collection of photographs.

For a truly glittering look, you can combine silver pieces with metallic decorations – for example, why not try wrapping silver-sprayed fabric flowers around candlesticks?

Unadorned modern silver frames are cleverly displayed with an antique-style vase to make a very pleasing arrangement. Ivory coloured roses look particularly good against the gleam of silver.

◀ *Silver-topped bottles* and jars make elegant accessories in a bathroom, creating a genteel mood and helping to soften the lines of modern fittings.

▼ *This frosted glass* perfume phial, with its art-deco style filigree silver decoration, would make a graceful adornment to any dressing table.

▲ *A collection of decorative silver trinket boxes* and a glass and silver perfume bottle make a stunning display on a blue damask cloth.

▶ *Ornate silver candelabras* add a touch of grandeur to a table setting, while delicately fashioned, bow-legged silver salt cellars and well polished cutlery complement the formal tone of the occasion.

A Festive Light

*Use flattering candlelight to set the scene for seasonal festivities,
romantic dinners and all manner of celebrations; and if you like the effect,
keep candles as a year-round feature in your home.*

C andlelight has a magical quality that can transform the most ordinary of settings into one brimming with warmth, romance and mystery. It instantly sets the mood for celebratory occasions and seasonal festivities, but there's no reason why you shouldn't use candles to add year-round atmosphere to your home.

You can use candles in many locations – on the dining table for intimate, low-level lighting, standing on a sideboard or mantelpiece to create a glowing display, or in wall-mounted candle sconces to light up a dull corner. Seek out stylish and original candle holders, or dream up your own display ideas

– set small candles in jewel-coloured glass tumblers, plant fat candles in rustic terracotta pots, or nestle a variety of differently sized candles in a bed of sparkling tinsel and Christmas baubles.

Put safety first when using candles and always take some precautions to guard against fire. Make sure the flame is well clear of flammable material and that the candles are firmly fixed in their holders, and out of the reach of young children. Above all, always extinguish candles when you go out or to bed, and never leave them burning in an unoccupied room. If you use candles regularly, you should have a smoke alarm.

Slender white candles in crystal and silver candlesticks set the scene for a celebratory meal. The crystal drops trimming two of the candlesticks add extra sparkle while small candles in starry containers create tiny pools of light.

◪ *A cheerful Santa Claus* and his snowy companion make jolly candle holders for the Christmas dinner table, or to display on the mantelpiece.

◪ *Pots of candles* are teamed with dried rose trees and Christmas baubles to create an extravagant and original display, bursting with colour and exciting textural contrasts.

◪ *Light the way* to the Christmas festivities with wall-mounted candle sconces, like these painted tin Christmas trees; their metallic surfaces reflect the candles' dancing flames.

◪ *A balanced arrangement* of tall white candles in slim glass candlesticks makes an elegant year-round display for this mantelshelf. An ivy and crystal-drop mantel trim adds a seasonal touch.

◪ *Trumpeting cherubs* fly atop this glinting metal candle holder, as the heat from the flames sets them spinning. The stand makes a delightful table centrepiece.

CANDLE LANTERNS

Indoors or out, the soft glow of a candle set in a lantern provides mood-invoking atmosphere. Protected by the glass of the lantern, the light is gently diffused, without flickering, to the surrounds.

F rom the flawless contours of an all-glass storm lantern to the sturdy tin and glass of a modern garden candle-lamp, candle lanterns have practical origins. Harking back to the days when candles were the only night-time light source, candle lanterns provided a safe and convenient way of lighting. Often with handles to make them easy to carry, firm bases to prevent them toppling over and a glass case to ensure the candle did not blow out in a sudden gust, household lanterns were a necessity. However, today lanterns are valued rather more for their decorative qualities than for any practical advantages, even when they are lit.

Unlit, they provide a perfect finishing touch to your home, whether they are hanging in the kitchen, living room or outdoors. Once lit, the atmospheric glow of the candlelamp has a year-round attraction. From the lighting up of your garden for a summer barbecue to the fairytale, festive look of Christmas, tin and glass candlelamps can twinkle out a cosy welcome to your guests.

Nostalgic tin and glass candlelamps welcome guests to outdoor summer festivities. Lit by night-lights, the lamps give off a surprisingly strong glow. The classic appeal of a hurricane lamp (right) never wanes.

◀ *An antique tin lantern* is the focal point of this global-theme display. The soft glow of the candle and foliage softens the severity of the collection of glass, marble and metals.

▼ *Capture the fading sunlight* of a midsummer's evening as the elongated shadows and candlelight mingle to provide the perfect setting for outdoor entertaining. The petal-filled base of the glass hurricane lamp and entwining ivy add colour to the summer haze.

◀ *Forget the fairy lights* next Christmas and create a festive welcome to your home by hanging miniature glass lamps on an outside tree. The light shining through the coloured glass gives a rich stained glass effect.

▼ *Cheer up* a gloomy winter's day by setting a shimmering collection of candlelamps on the mantelpiece to create a romantic, magical feeling in the room.

METAL CANDLEHOLDERS

Flickering candles are one of the most magical ways of setting the scene for a celebration. Display them to best effect in gleaming metal holders made from discarded tin cans or metal foil.

T he soft glow of candlelight has a magic all its own – there's nothing quite like it for adding a festive touch to a special table setting or garden party. Its dancing flames are shown off to best effect by glinting metal holders which reflect their warm glow – from the gleaming sparkle of silver candlesticks to the homey, softer sheen of tin lanterns, wall sconces and chambersticks.

At the more modest end of the scale, many of the most attractive candleholders are made from decorative tinware, using techniques which you can adapt to create your own designs. It's satisfying to use recycled metal containers, such as old paint tins and food cans, as your starting point.

Apart from tinsnips, available from do-it-yourself stores, you don't need any special tools and equipment – you cut up the containers with the snips, beat them flat with a hammer and bend them into shape with pliers. Decorative metal foil, available from art and craft suppliers, is even easier to use as you can cut it with sharp scissors and it easily twists into shape.

Decorate the holders by punching holes through the metal with a hammer and nail, or hammering the nails just partway in, without piercing, to create raised designs. For extra ornamentation, glue on glass beads, sequins and other embellishments.

It's simple to turn old metal containers into hanging lanterns. Pierce holes in the sides to let the candlelight shine through and decorate with gloss or enamel paint – bright stripes in primary colours look effective.

MAKING A TIN LANTERN

Tin lanterns are ideal for lighting a garden as they protect the candle flames from draughts. The punched hole patterns are practical as well as decorative, allowing the flame to shine through. To make a lantern you need a large empty paint tin for the base and any container made from soft metal that can be cut with tinsnips for the lid – an empty, and clean, motor oil can or jumbo-sized coffee tin is ideal. Always wear protective gloves when cutting metal as the edges are razor sharp.

For a decorative finish, pierce holes in the lantern with square or round nails and cut long dashes with an old wood chisel. Start by sketching designs on paper; you'll be surprised how many different patterns you can create from a combination of dots and dashes. For speed in transferring a symmetrical pattern, fold over the paper lengthways and draw a pattern over one half, then use a pin to transfer the marks to the other half.

1 Marking out the pattern Remove the handle from the paint tin. Measure the height and circumference of the tin and cut out a rectangle of brown paper to the same size. Mark off a 2.5cm (1in) border along the top and bottom edges. Draw a pattern of dots and dashes between these lines with a felt tip pen.

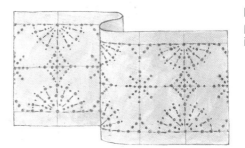

2 Punching the tin Tightly pack the tin with earth or sand and hammer down the lid. Wrap the pattern round the tin and fix with masking tape. Use a hammer and nails of varying sizes to punch holes through both the pattern and tin at each dot mark. Then use a hammer and an old wood chisel to cut the dashes. Remove the pattern and empty out earth or sand.

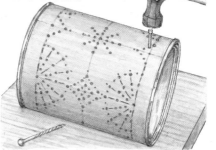

3 Cutting out the lid Open out the motor oil can by removing the top and bottom with tinsnips and cutting down the side seam. Draw a circle twice the diameter of the paint tin on the metal with compasses and felt tip pen. Within this, draw a second circle 2.5cm (1in) smaller than the first, and a third circle 7.5cm (3in) diameter. Divide into quarter sections. Cut out the large circle with tinsnips. Then cut out one quarter section and the central 7.5cm (3in) circle. Keep the surplus metal for the handle.

4 Decorating the lid Using a large coin as a template, draw a scallop pattern round the outside edge of the lid and cut it out with the tinsnips. Protecting your work surface with a scrap of wood, pierce a few punched hole patterns in the lid. Curl back the two straight ends of the lid with pliers, reversing the curl on one so they interlock. Hammer the interlocked edges flat.

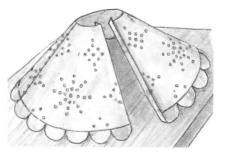

5 Making the handle Use the central 7.5cm (3in) circle and cut another strip of metal 4cm (1½in) by 20cm (8in). Cut long, tapered tails at both ends of the strip and bend back the long edges by 6mm (¼in). Cut a slit in the centre of the circle just wide enough to fit the tails through. Ripple the circle by bending the edges over a nail.

6 Assembling the lantern Push the tails through the slit in the circle, and through the hole in the top of the lid. Bend back the tails on the underside of the lid to secure the handle. Spray the lantern and lid inside and out with matt black paint. When dry, attach the lid to the paint tin with small pieces of bent wire, pushing them through punched holes in both the tin and the lid and twisting the ends together. To insert a candle, untwist the wire and secure candle with a little melted wax. Light the candle and wire the lid back on.

▶ *Practise the art of recycling by transforming an old paint tin into a charming punched hole candle lantern, complete with handle so that it can be hung up to add sparkle to any special occasion.*

WORKING WITH METAL FOIL

Metal foil is available from craft suppliers in a variety of different colours and thicknesses. It is far more substantial than the aluminium foil used in the kitchen. Small twists of foil can be glued to a candleholder made from recycled metal; or you can use it on its own to make delicate, lightweight decorations like the candle crowns and Christmas wall sconce shown on this page.

For projects like these, choose a foil you can cut to shape easily with household scissors. Small embroidery scissors are particularly useful when cutting out intricate filagree-style shapes.

The metal foil is very soft so you can create interesting textures by buffing areas with steel wool or by pressing lines on the surface with a knitting needle. Hammer nails lightly into the back for an embossed effect on the front, or push out light-diffusing patterns with a bradawl.

▶ You can make a pretty wall sconce similar to the one shown here from a sheet of metal foil and a small clip-on Christmas tree candleholder. Cut the tree and the curved support from one piece of foil, reinforcing the support by bending the cut edges into the centre. Emboss the tree by pushing a variety of nails and screw heads into the back. Bend the support into shape and clip the candleholder on top.

▼ Brighten up a buffet supper with twinkling candle crowns. Cut the crowns out of metal foil and decorate them with punched hole patterns pierced with a bradawl. Gently bend the flat shapes into cylinders and secure the overlapped edges with brass paper fasteners. For a glittering jewel-like quality, glue large coloured glass beads behind some of the holes. Set the candles on saucers and cover them with the crowns.

CANDLEMAKING

Simple and inexpensive to make, candles in flower pots or shells and little floating flowers of wax add an appealing glow to outdoor evenings – and, with added scent, ward off hungry insects too.

The entrancing light of candle flames creates an instant atmosphere in any environment, informal or formal. With their infinite versatility – adding a sense of occasion to any meal, a cosy glow on a chilly winters' evening or setting a romantic mood – candles are rarely out of place. Grouped together they are even more captivating, but can prove an expensive treat. A simple, less extravagant alternative is to make your own.

The candles shown here and on the following pages are easy and inexpensive to make, requiring a few candlemaking materials and some basic cooking utensils. The results are exclusive candles, shaped, coloured and perfumed to suit a theme, colour-scheme or nose, but without a price tag that makes them an extravagance you feel you should reserve for celebrations and holidays.

Set adrift on water and bobbing among flower petals, floating candles moulded in tiny cake tins create a dreamy display for a table centrepiece or a garden water feature. By experiment and careful mixing you can concoct a candle colour palette to match your tableware or flowers in bloom. Quick to make en-masse, you can have fun creating seasonal floating candles – perhaps some stars for Christmas, or heart shapes for a romantic Valentines' supper.

Back on dry land, you can fill enamel mugs, tin cans and coconut shells with wax to make container candles of all shapes and sizes. For a garden party you could make container candles in terracotta flowerpots or miniature galvanized metal pails and use them to line paths and patios. And, when eventually the candle expires, simply melt some more wax and refill the containers.

Drifting in a garden pool, these floating candles look very natural – like flickering water lilies, with their soft lights reflected subtly across the water.

MAKING CANDLES

Candlemaking is a rewarding and surprisingly simple craft that requires only a few inexpensive raw materials and some basic kitchen utensils. Using various shaped containers and moulds – bought or found – and experimenting with different colours and perfumes, you can create candles to brighten every day of the year.

EQUIPMENT

Wax The type of wax commonly used for candlemaking is *paraffin wax*. It is an odourless, white wax which melts at 40-71°C (104-160°F) and is usually sold in pellet form. *Beeswax* is an attractive alternative with a creamy colour, distinct honey perfume and a longer burning time, but it is more expensive. To improve the burning time of paraffin wax, add five per cent beeswax.

Stearin is often mixed with molten paraffin wax to improve the candle burning quality and to shrink the wax slightly so it's easier to remove from a mould. It's not used for container candles because it makes the wax shrink away from the sides of the container. If using stearin, melt it with the wax in a ratio of one part stearin to ten parts wax. You can buy *prepared paraffin wax* with stearin added.

Wax dyes, in solid or powder form, are used to colour wax. You can mix colours in much the same way as paint, building up the colour gradually and combining dyes. *Wax crayons* can also be melted down to colour wax, or

you can buy ready-coloured prepared wax.

Wax perfumes can be added to molten wax, to provide a scent when the candle is burnt. Some essential oils can also be added, but test them before adding to a batch of candles – some have a bitter smell when burnt. Add a few drops of the perfume when the wax reaches 75°C (167°F), and do not heat above this temperature.

Wicks carry the vapour from the molten candle wax to the flame. For the candle to burn well you need to use the correct type and size of wick; container and floating candles, for example, need particular types of wick. Wick sizes are quoted according to the final candle diameter; for example, a 5cm (2in) diameter candle requires a 5cm (2in) wick. The wick must stand about 2-3cm (¾-1¼in) above the candle surface, otherwise the flame is likely to be extinguished in the molten wax.

Wick sustainers, or supports, are metal discs used to anchor the wick in container candles. **Double boilers**, made of aluminium or stainless steel, are best for melting wax. Alternatively, though the wax does not melt as evenly, you can melt it in a heatproof bowl placed over a saucepan of water. Once you have poured out the wax, wipe off surplus wax from the boiler with a dry kitchen towel.

Wax or **cooking thermometers** with a 38-108°C (100-226°F) range, indicate when the wax reaches the right temperature.

BASIC TECHNIQUES

How much wax? To calculate how much cold wax you need for making candles in containers or moulds, fill the container or mould with water to the required level, then transfer the water into a measuring jug. For each 100ml (3½fl oz) of water you need 90g (3oz) of cold wax.

Colouring the wax If using stearin, add dye to the melted stearin before adding the paraffin wax, otherwise add dye directly to the melted wax. Melt the stearin or wax then, mixing thoroughly with an old spoon, add a small amount of wax dye, coloured crayon or ready-coloured wax until you achieve the desired colour. To test the colour, allow a drop of molten wax to set on a sheet of greaseproof paper. Add more dye if necessary.

Priming the wick Melt a small amount of paraffin wax in the top pan of a double boiler until it reaches 71°C (160°F). Fold a wick in half; holding it at the fold, dip the wick in the molten wax. Allow to soak for one minute then lift out, pull straight and lay to cool on a sheet of greaseproof paper.

CONTAINER CANDLES

You can fill all sorts of containers with wax to make candles, from seashells and plant pots to old glasses and teacups. Whatever container you choose, you must ensure it is clean and dry before pouring in the wax. If you are using a terracotta pot with a drainage hole, seal the hole first with a few drops of wax. It's easier to insert the wick into very shallow containers, such as shells, while the wax is cooling: see step 4, *Floating Candles*.

1 **Melting the wax** See *How much wax?* (opposite) to calculate how much cold wax you need. Using weighing scales, measure out this amount of cold wax and transfer to the top pan of a double boiler. Melt the wax and, mixing thoroughly with a wooden spoon, add the wax dye to get the colour desired. Continue heating the wax gently.

2 **Securing the wicks** After *Priming the wick* (see opposite) cut a length of wick about 5cm (2in) longer than the height of the container. Thread one end of the wick through a wick sustainer. Wind the other end around a skewer and rest this across the top of the container, so the wick sustainer lies centrally at the base of the container. Stand the container in a bowl of cold water filled to the final height of the wax, placing a weight on top of the container if it floats.

3 **Pouring the wax** Test the temperature of the wax. If adding perfume, stop heating when the temperature reaches 75°C (167°F); otherwise heat to 82°C (180°F). Start pouring wax into the container, taking care not to dislodge the wick. Continue pouring to about 1.2cm (½in) below the final candle height.

4 **Finishing off** Leave to cool for about one hour – in this time the wax shrinks away from the wick, forming a well. Prick the surface of the wax with a needle to release any bubbles, then reheat the unused wax and top up the candle. Leave to cool for 1-2 hours, then remove the skewer and trim the wick to about 2cm (¾in).

🔺 *Flowerpot candles are perfect for illuminating an outdoor gathering. Add a few drops of citronella oil to the melted wax to help ward off mosquitoes and midges and fill the wax to just below the rim so the flame is protected from draughts and breezes.*

🔽 *As long as you take care when pouring the hot, melted wax, turning empty whelk, limpet and cockle shells into small novelty candles is quite simple. Once the wax has solidified slightly, you can press in the wicks as you do when making floating candles (see the following page).*

FLOATING CANDLES

Wax floats in water and you can take advantage of this by making floating candles. Small, shallow candles with a central wick float and burn best. You need smooth-sided moulds which are wider at the top than the base, so the candles are easy to remove. Choose moulds with interesting outlines, because this is the shape you see when the candle is floating in water. Metal brioche bun and petit four tins with prettily scalloped edges are ideal.

To make sure that the candle comes away from the mould quite freely, you need to add stearin to the wax so it shrinks away from the mould. Measure the wax, prime the wicks and colour and perfume the candles, if desired, as previously described.

YOU WILL NEED

- ❖ SMALL MOULDS
- ❖ PARAFFIN WAX
- ❖ STEARIN
- ❖ MEASURING JUG AND SCALES
- ❖ DOUBLE BOILER
- ❖ WOODEN SPOON
- ❖ WAX OR COOKING THERMOMETER, 38-108°C (100-226°F)
- ❖ WAX DYE (optional)
- ❖ CANDLE PERFUME (optional)
- ❖ FLOATING CANDLE WICKS
- ❖ OLD NEEDLE
- ❖ BOWL
- ❖ WEIGHTS (optional)

▶ *A group of floating candles burning together creates a flickering pool of light. If displayed in a glass bowl, keep the water level close to the rim so that there is no danger of the glass cracking.*

1 Melting the wax Fill the moulds with water to calculate how much cold wax you need. Measure this amount of wax and put to one side. Divide the weight of cold wax by 10 and measure out this amount of stearin. Melt the stearin in a double boiler and, mixing thoroughly, add wax dye to colour. Add the wax and continue heating gently.

2 Pouring the wax Prime the wicks. Stand the moulds in a shallow bowl of cold water, weighting them down if they float. When the wax reaches 82°C (180°F) remove the pan from the heat. Carefully pour the wax into the moulds, filling them to just below the rim.

3 Topping up the moulds Tap the sides of the moulds to release any air bubbles. Allow to cool until the wax has just started to set. Prick the surface of the wax with an old needle to release any bubbles, then reheat the unused wax in the top of the double boiler and carefully top up the moulds.

4 Inserting the wicks Leave until the wax has solidified slightly but is still soft. Cut pieces of wick about 2.5cm (1in) longer than the depth of the candles. Push the wicks into the centre of the wax. Leave until set then turn out the candles and trim the wicks to 1-2cm (³⁄₈-³⁄₄in).

Index

ACKNOWLEDGEMENTS

Photographs: 7 Ikea, 8(tl) EWA/Richard Davies, (cl) Spur Shelving, (bl) Worldwide Syndication, 8-9(t) Abode, (bc) Worldwide Syndication, 9(br) Spur Shelving, 10(tl,b) Robert Harding Syndication/IPC Magazines, (tr) Worldwide Syndication, 11(tl) EWA, (tr) EWA/Rodney Hyett, 12(t) Ikea, (bl) Habitat, (br) Spur Shelving, 13 Robert Harding Syndication/IPC Magazines, 14-16 EM/Graham Rae, 16(bl) Robert Harding Syndication/IPC Magazines, 17 Dulux, 18(tl) EWA/Andreas von Einsiedel, (tr) Robert Harding Syndication/IPC Magazines, (bl) Doulton Bathrooms, (br) Marie Claire Idées/Chabaneix/Chabaneix, 19 Robert Harding Syndication/IPC Magazines, 20-21 Home Flair, 22(l) Arcaid/Geoff Lung, (r) EWA/Spike Powell, 23 Wood Brothers, 24 EM/Steve Tanner, 25-26 Home Flair, 27 Robert Harding Syndication/IPC Magazines, 28(tl) International Interiors, (tr,bl) Robert Harding Syndication/IPC Magazines, 29 Ariadne, 30(t) EWA/Spike Powell, (c,b) Robert Harding Syndication/IPC Magazines, 31 Ariadne, 32(tl) Ikea, (tr) Doehet Zelf, (b) Ariadne, 33 Marie Claire Idées/Schwartz/Thiebaut-Morelle, 34(tl) Robert Harding Syndication/IPC Magazines, (tr) EWA/Bryan/Jaisay, (b) Marie Claire Idées/Hussenot/Chastres/Lancrenon, 35 Robert Harding Syndication/IPC Magazines, 36(tl,br) Robert Harding Syndication/IPC Magazines, (tr) EWA/Michael Crockett, (bl) Stag Minstrel, 37 Robert Harding Syndication/IPC Magazines, 38(tl) Laura Ashley, (bl) Habitat, (br) FTE Designs, 39 Robert Harding Syndication/IPC Magazines, 40(t,bl) Robert Harding Syndication/IPC Magazines, (b) Dorma, 41 Abode, 42(t,cr) Robert Harding Syndication/IPC Magazines, (bl) Harlequin Fabrics and Wallcoverings, (br) Arcaid/Simon Kelly, 43 Robert Harding Syndication/IPC Magazines, 44(tl) EWA/Richard Davies, (tr) Worldwide Syndication, (b) Ikea, 45 EWA/Andreas von Einsiedel, 46(t) Robert Harding Syndication/IPC Magazines, (tr) EWA/Andreas von Einsiedel, (bl) EWA/Neil Lorimer, (br) EM/Martin Chaffer, 47 Robert Harding Syndication/IPC Magazines, 48(tl) Robert Harding Syndication/IPC Magazines, (tr,bl) Ariadne, (br) EM/Graham Rae, 49 Ariadne, 50-51

EM/Steve Tanner, 52 Ariadne, 53-56 Robert Harding Syndication/IPC Magazines, 57 Worldwide Syndication, 58(t) Worldwide Syndication, (c,bl) Robert Harding Syndication/IPC Magazines, (br) EWA/Shona Wood, 59 Marie Claire Idées/Hussenot/Lancrenon/Chombart, 61-62 EM/Graham Rae, 63 EWA/Tom Leighton, 64(t,bl) Robert Harding Syndication/IPC Magazines, (br) EWA/Brian Harrison, 65 EWA/Michael Dunne, 66(tl,br) Robert Harding Syndication/IPC Magazines, (tr) EWA, (bl) EWA/Michael Dunne, 67 EM/Adrian Taylor, 68(tl) EWA/Nadia MacKenzie, (tr,b) Robert Harding Syndication/IPC Magazines, 69-72 EM/Paul Bricknell, 73 EM/Graham Rae, 75 Belle, (inset) EM/Graham Rae, 76(tl) EM/Simon Page-Ritchie, (tc) Reptile Tiles, (tr,cl) EM/Graham Rae, (cr) The English Stamp Co, (b) Robert Harding Syndication/IPC Magazines, 77 Robert Harding Syndication/IPC Magazines, 78(tl) Robert Harding Syndication/IPC Magazines, (tr) Marie Claire Idées/Chabaneix/Chabaneix/Harnon, (bl) Home Flair, (br) Marie Claire Idées/Chabaneix/Chabaneix/Sitaud, 79 Robert Harding Syndication/IPC Magazines, 80(t) Robert Harding Syndication/IPC Magazines, (bl) Pébéo, (br) Emma Bridgewater, 81 Robert Harding Syndication/IPC Magazines, 82(t) Marie Claire Idées/Chabaneix/Chabaneix/Richard, (cl) EM/Graham Rae, (bl) Robert Harding Syndication/IPC Magazines, (br) Romo Ltd, 83 PWA International, 84 Robert Harding Syndication/IPC Magazines, 85 Robert Harding Syndication/IPC Magazines, 86(tl) Abode, (tr) Ehrman, (bl) Jane Churchill, (br) Abode, 87(t) Ariadne, (b) Robert Harding Syndication/IPC Magazines, 88(t,bl) Robert Harding Syndication/IPC Magazines, (br) Ariadne, 89 Robert Harding Syndication/IPC Magazines, 90(l) Robert Harding Syndication/IPC Magazines, (tr) Jolly Red, (c,br) EM/Simon Page-Ritchie, (cr) Marie Claire Idées/Chabaneix, 91 Robert Harding Syndication/IPC Magazines, 92(tl) The Garden Picture Library/Linda Burgess, (tr) EWA/Di Lewis, (bl) Marie Claire Idées/Giaume/Lancrenon, (br) Arcaid/Rodney Weiland, 93 Robert Harding Syndication/IPC Magazines, 94(l,br) Robert Harding Syndication/IPC Magazines, (tr) EM/Graham Rae, 95 Robert Harding Syndication/IPC Magazines, 96(t) Robert Harding Syndication/IPC Magazines, (cr) Home

Flair, (bl) Ariande, (br) EM/Steve Tanner, 97 Marie Claire Idées/Chabaneix/Chabaneix, 98(tl) Abode, (tr) EM/Graham Rae, (bl) Marie Claire Maison/Beaufre/Billaud, (br) Doehet Zelf, 99 Home Flair, 100(t) Home Flair, (bl) EWA/Spike Powell, (br) EWA/Rodney Hyett, 101 Robert Harding Syndication/IPC Magazines, 102(tl) EWA/Di Lewis, (tr) EM/Steve Tanner, (bl) Tabbycat, (br) EM/Mark Wood, 103 Robert Harding Syndication/IPC Magazines, 104(tl) EWA/Spike Powell, (c,br) Robert Harding Syndication/IPC Magazines, 105 Marie Claire Idées/Hussenot/Chastres, 106(tl) EWA/Neil Lorimer, (tr) Robert Harding Syndication/IPC Magazines, (bl) Ariadne, (br) EM/Laura Wickenden, 107 Marie O'Hara, 108(tl) Abode, (tr) EWA/Di Lewis, (b) Robert Harding Syndication/IPC Magazines, 109 Robert Harding Syndication/IPC Magazines, 110(tl) Boys Syndication, (tr) Robert Harding Syndication/IPC Magazines, (bl) Ariadne, (br) EM/Simon Page-Ritchie, 111 EWA/Nadia MacKenzie, 112(tl) Robert Harding Syndication/IPC Magazines, (tr,l) Past Times, (br) Marie Claire Idées/Schwartz/Lancrenon, 113 Robert Harding Syndication/IPC Magazines, 114(t) Robert Harding Syndication/IPC Magazines, (bl) EM/Mark Wood, (br) EWA/Andreas von Einsiedel, 115 Robert Harding Syndication/IPC Magazines, 116(tl) Argos, (r) Robert Harding Syndication/IPC Magazines, (cl) The Pier, (bl) EM/Graham Rae, 117(t) Worldwide Syndication, (b) Robert Harding Syndication/IPC Magazines, 118(t) Marie Claire Maison/Verger/Comte, (cl) Past Times, (cr) Robert Harding Syndication/IPC Magazines, (b) Marie Claire Maison/Bailhache/Bayle, 119 Marie Claire Idées/Chabaneix/Harnon, 121 Robert Harding Syndication/IPC Magazines, 122(t) Robert Harding Syndication/IPC Magazines, (b) Marie Claire Idées/Chabaneix/Chabaneix, 123 Robert Harding Syndication/IPC Magazines, 124-126 EM/Graham Rae.

Illustrations: 14-15 Aziz Khan, 24 Sally Holmes, 50-56 John Hutchinson, 60-62 Coral Mula, 70-74 Sally Holmes, 120 Sally Holmes, 124-126 Coral Mula.